Preface

I have been very fortunate to meet all the interesting characters and wonderful people along the paths I have chosen. My life has been rich in experiences. I want to thank God for my blessings, and my family and friends for their help and patience.

The Cow Whisperer has been out quite a few years now and I meet people all the time who tell me how hard they laughed over some of the stories. I hope this book makes you laugh too.

Dances with Hooves

By Skip Halmes

This book is dedicated to my girl,

Katie

Copyright © 2007 by Skip Halmes

Illustrations Copyright © 2007 by
R Tom Gilleon

Cover illustration photo copyright of
Gail Molyneaux Photographics 2006

Cover illustration is of Jake Halmes
on "Knot Head" of Red Eye Rodeo

Three Forks Montana 2006

Bud and Charlie

Charlie and Bud were crabby old salts who had been spawned in the Great Depression. They had gone to the same grade school and weren't about to be outdone by the other. Both had been mad at pretty much everyone and about everything for about the last twenty years. To hear them tell it, the trail had been uphill to school both ways, it snowed more, and the horses had all bucked harder. They never gave an inch and were highly skeptical of any new idea or anyone born after nineteen fifty. Adversity was their mother, and according to them, anyone suffering tribulation probably deserved that, and a lot more. They consistently prophesized hard times, so nothing cheered them up more than a break in the cattle market, a prolonged drought, or some young cowboy's folly. The years had taken quite a toll on their hearing so they yelled at each other. Their misconstrued conversations were broadcast to everyone within twenty yards.

Charlie had been a rancher and cattle buyer all his life. He always cursed high interest rates and the present administration. His best years for profit and health had been the sixties. Those were the good old days that he used to gauge the rest of his life. It rained more, the cattle were better, people were nicer, etc. Charlie always wore a silver belly Stetson with a high crown and the brim bent up like a taco. I don't think he ever changed his pants size but just moved his Lee jeans a little lower over the years so that they drooped under his formidable potbelly.

Even though now he had plenty of wealth, he saved every penny and pickle jar, never ever tipped, and whined about a fifty-cent cup of coffee that came with endless refills. His dress style was like a country western singer from the seventies, and he always sported a black silk scarf around his neck. Today, like most days, he was chewing a toothpick and wearing a nylon down-filled jacket with a few cigarette burns on the sleeves.

Bud was seventy-five and he had gone broke farming in 1988. He wore a faded brown duck coat with badly frayed greasy cuffs. Deep lines in his face born of weather and worry surrounded some glasses specked from welding and a reddening nose. His face rarely betrayed any expression, but if you watched closely his light blue eyes sparkled when he heard a good joke or something else that pleased him - like a big correction in the stock market or a plague of locusts. He lived mostly on Social Security and some odd jobs like fencing or some night calving for the local ranchers. He was a little too proud to work for Charlie. He wore a cap that advertised some brand of cattle wormer that was so old and dirty you couldn't tell what the original color might have been. He started the daily banter that he and Charlie had gone through at least four times a week for the last twenty years. Bud was in their spot. The same table and at our local café, Hungry Herb's Hangout, and he asked Charlie the same way he always got the banter rolling.

"How's it going today?"

"Still fightin' it," Charlie said.

When Charlie talked, it sounded like an old dog growling. The more excited or nervous he got the faster his toothpick darted around.

"Well, you always did like the battle more than the victory."
They both drank some coffee.

Your ex–wife told me that," Bud said.

Nola or Iris?" Charlie asked with an eyebrow raised.

Both of em'," Bud frowned.

"You're a helluva' one to talk to me about ex-wives," Charlie grumbled.

"I'm just sayin'," Bud replied.

"Do you know Nola went to town last week to buy the same kind of car as Iris has?" Charlie said. "It's exactly the same kind but a different color. Those women are both scared to death that the other one will look like she's doing better or got something newer than the other one."

"How'd you find that out?" Bud inquired after slurping his coffee.

"She called me one night," Charlie whispered softly.

"One nut! Why'd she call you one nut?" Bud asked.

"She wanted to tell me about her new Lexus, I think," Charlie said.

"I thought she was feeling better now. Where did she get apoplexies?" Bud asked.

"From that car dealer that's advertising on TV all the time up in Great Falls," Charlie said.

"When did she start seeing that guy?" Bud asked.

"She aint' as far as I know," Charlie said.

He drank some more coffee and had a happy thought.

"All my exes drive a Lexus."

"Isn't there a song about that?" Bud recalled.

The café was busy that morning and they both sized up the rest of the morning patrons.

"Ex-wives and Democrats, they'll be the end of all of us," Charlie admitted.

"By God, it's been a good wet year so far." Bud said, trying to change the subject.

"That just means we're one year closer to one of those really bad dry sons-a-bitches," Charlie said with a grudge.

"My dad told me that a couple times he was so thirsty that he drank the muddy water out of a hoof print," Bud said.

"Hell, that's nothin'. I was so thirsty once that I drank the piss out of a grizzly track -- with the bear still in it!" Charlie growled.

Bud rolled his eyes and took a long drink of coffee. Then he asked, "How are the calves you bought from the Dearborn Ranch doing?"

"They're good steers but, by God, I'm gonna' lose a hundred bucks a head on this last set I'm feedin' down in Iowa. Those big packers got this thing right where they want it," Charlie said. "They won't be happy till we're all broke and then they'll be the only ones feedin' any cattle. They'll control the whole damn thing pretty soon."

Bud shook his head, "You guys sure weren't bitchin' when these cattle were so high a couple years ago. Everyone was buying new pickups and eatin' out all the time."

"A guy's got to have one of those years once in awhile to keep afloat and make up for all the wrecks and the high price of everything," Charlie replied wiping a dribble off his chin.

"Well, I noticed you're struggling along well enough to get another new Cadillac," Bud countered. "Things can't be too bad."

Charlie's spartan breakfast came and he started working on it.

"Well, this new one is supposed to get better mileage. Gas is gonna' be three dollars a gallon by summer and I can't afford much of that. The way this cow business is going a guy has to save money any way you can," Charlie grumbled.

"Is that why you order oatmeal every morning for breakfast?" Bud questioned.

Charlie took the spoon out of his mouth and snorted, "Hell no! I like oatmeal. I've been eatin' it since I was weaned."

"At least you were lucky enough to have oatmeal. Hell, all we had was choke cherries and hardtack - and we were damn glad to have it. For dinner my mom used to just send me down to the brush by the creek for wild berries, and then awhile later she would send my big sister with a switch to beat me off 'em," Bud licked his lips. "That way I wouldn't eat 'em all and there would be some left for the next night."

"Well, you guys could afford that pet dog, Tumbleweed. All we had was a pet rattlesnake," Charlie grumbled.

"Your folks let you have a pet rattlesnake?"

Charlie nodded slowly in affirmation.

"You lucky bastard! We didn't have no dog. We couldn't afford one. Our pet *was* a tumbleweed, and I got teased plenty about that at show and tell. My sister used to lead it around and taught it to roll over."

They both paused to stare at a pretty school teacher wearing spandex walking briskly by the café window.

"Well, one thing I've figured out over the years is," Bud paused and rubbed his chin, "That it's a hell of lot better to inherit a ranch than it is to work on one."

Charlie noticed his cup was empty and gave a hearty wave to the busy waitress for their third refill. A dour girl wearing tie-dyed bib overalls scurried over, refilled their cups, and lisped something that sounded like cheap sunny beaches.

"I can never understand a thing that girl of Herb's says," Charlie said shaking his head. "It's like she's got a mouthfull of mush and she's always dartin' around in here like a hopped-up weasel."

"Well she got her tongue pierced over in that Hippy College at Missoula, and I think she spent all four years over there smoking pot. When she came home, she was so dopey she just moped around in her sweatsuit all day and then watched TV till late at night for six months in a row," Bud looked around and then lowered his voice. "Her dad told me she has some syndrome. Adult children of co-dependent Catholics or some other B.S. deal like that. He made her take this job while she is waiting for her book to get published."

"Her book?" Charlie asked.

"It's about Indian love poems or some other crap. Anyway, now she sucks down that espresso all day to keep perked up. It kinda' keeps her on an even keel I guess."

"What did she go to college for? What's she wanna' be?" Charlie asked.

"She took acting lessons." Bud said. "Her mom said she wants to be a thespian."

Charlie shook his head and bit down on his toothpick.

"I always figured she might swing from both sides of the plate. But isn't she goin' out with that new cowboy from the sixes with the long moustache and the big hat."

"That's what I thought, too, but who knows. You know that guy's in the hospital for the third time this year," Bud said.

"The buckaroo from Missoree? -- Who tucks his pants inside those high-topped boots of his," Charlie chuckled.

"Yup that's him." Bud said. "All those guys bug me. Every time I see some guy wobbling around on high-heeled boots doing a Tex Ritter imitation and looking disoriented, I figure it's probably because he got kicked out of Nevada. I think they might have laws down there against impersonating cowboys. All hat and no cattle is what I always say."

Charlie shook his head and worked his toothpick around to the other side of his mouth. "I've figured out that most of the time if you need some help, you are way ahead to pick the guy wearing a ball cap and some Whites Packers or tennis shoes," Charlie advised.

"I know," Bud began with a grin, "Our neighbor, Bob Lemire, who works over there on the Dana ranch, said they hired this fellow and he told me the guy's big black hat was shaped like someone had been hitting him in the head with sticks. After he had worked with him some, he said that's probably what happened. Bob asked him once how he liked the horses on this ranch compared to the last place he worked."

Bud changed his voice trying to imitate the poor fellow. He drawled, *'They aint throwed' nothing too tough at me yet. A horse in my string they call Patches is pretty woofie' but I aint' had no trouble gettin' the kinks out of him.'*

Charlie hit his hand on the table. "Good God! I know that old horse. It's that roan mare that the widow Zurich rode."

"That's the one, and I know that ranch doesn't keep any bronky' horses around at all. Patches is the kind of horse you'd let the kids ride bareback to get in the milk cow. The pony is basically retired and usually not ambitious enough to jump over a garden hose on a spring morning," Bud took a big drink of coffee and went on.

"I knew it wouldn't be too long before that fellow got in his own way, and the last I heard, nurses were feedin' him lunch with a straw."

"Did he get his chinks wound up in the four-wheeler?" Charlie slid the toothpick to his other side of the mouth. "I guess that's what happened before."

"No, it's even better." Bud beamed.

"I thought maybe he got those big spur rowels hung on the tractor clutch," Charlie snickered.

"Wasn't that either. Him and that fat old horse that you sold them last year got in a big wreck," Bud beamed with one eye brow raised.

"No way! That horse wouldn't run if you set his tail on fire. That's why I sold him. That horse was too pokey for even me. I can't believe it!" Charlie said.

"The way I hear, it wasn't really the horse's fault." Bud said, and looked out longingly again at the pretty teacher coming back from her walk.

"That makes sense. By God, when I was young we used to tie those bad ones down and spit tobacco juice in their eye," Charlie said.

"What for?" Bud asked.

"Show em' whose boss. They were some bad sombitches, too. Took forever to get em gentle."

"Imagine that," Bud said and rolled his eyes.

"Well, are ya' gonna' tell me what happened or make me guess?" Charlie persisted. He leaned in close to hear every detail.

"The story I got was, that he was trying to use that eighty-foot lariat of his to catch a calf. Those long buckaroo reins he uses, loop around in one piece and go back into his belt. On top of that I guess he had a piggin' string and a long bull whip strapped to his saddle, too. I think it was just too much rope and stuff for him to keep track of," Bud chuckled as he wiped his glasses

"So how did he get hurt?" Charlie asked again. "What the hell happened?"

"Well, I guess he caught the calf, dallied the tail of his whip by mistake, and then the coils of his catch rope just got tangled up in that loop-around rein deal he was usin' or somthin'. They say he was pleading with his maker and just begging the horse to slow up at the top of his lungs." Taking another gulp, Bud continued, "That just made the calf run faster, which just pulled harder on his loop around reins. So basically the calf was leading the horse across the prairie about a hundred miles an hour, and then I guess he either panicked or tried to save his hat."

"What do ya' mean save his hat?" Charlie asked dropping his jaw and losing his toothpick.

"I think he was trying to stop his horse, but I guess he grabbed the stampede string hooked to his hat instead of his reins." Bud said. "The faster that old horse went, the harder he pulled, and I think he just choked himself plumb out. He hasn't quite come around yet. All he has said so far is *Capriola's*."

Grabbing another toothpick, Charlie asked, "Ya think he'll be OK or ever ride again?"

Bud explained finishing the story, "Well, as you can imagine, as stupid as he was, it's gonna' be pretty hard to determine perceptible brain damage, and the horse wreck destroyed and scattered all his fancy gear from hell to breakfast. They say it completely ruined his saddle and tore off both jingle-bobs."

"That's probably best. Those guys shouldn't have kids anyway."

Amos 3:3

Secret Sam

When I was nine I suffered an identity crisis. I couldn't decide if I was going to be a professional hunter or an international spy. I made my own spy kit by covering the outside of an old suit case with black electrical tape. I filled it with play pistols, a notebook, road maps, my pocket knife and other spy stuff. I had twine to tie up double agents, some fire crackers for munitions, and extra caps for my pistol. I practiced my karate and tried to talk like Bond --James Bond. At that time there was also a television series about an international adventurer who captured dangerous animals and kissed beautiful women, "Bring em' Back Alive Frank Buck". I was torn as to which path I should follow.

As you know, I grew up way out in the country. So a major problem was that there wasn't much to spy on. I used to sneak over to do surveillance on my grandma's pigs and I rigged booby traps around the ranch. The pigs were quite ambivalent about my stakeout and evidently there weren't many boobies in the country because I never caught one. I did manage to catch the hired man one time in a snare that I had rigged with a strong willow tree.

I was always trying to sneak up on my big sister Caren, but she was too wary for me. She usually heard or saw me before I could do any proper espionage. For lack of anything more spylike, I decided I might as well switch to an assassin mode and shoot her with my cork gun.

On this particular day she was sitting on a kitchen stool talking to her friend and eating spaghetti. My opportunity was for a close attack. Those old pop guns didn't have much range. So, on this mission I got right up under her. I put the end of it right up to her hind pocket and gave her both barrels. I had replaced the corks with straight pins. Wow! It was an incident vivid enough that I am still impressed by the altitude and volume of her reaction. We never did get all the noodles off the ceiling. The mission had required me to blow my cover, however, and I was subjected to an interrogation process that involved my mother and a wooden spoon. At the time I argued the punishment would not have passed muster with the articles of the Geneva Convention. I ended up doing some hard time and a stretch of solitary confinement.

Even after discipline and house arrest, I was driven to proceed with my undercover activities. I made a spy radio out of a little piece of wood and drew a speaker and dials on the front. I kept this in my shirt pocket and reported my progress and location to headquarters at regular intervals. I often changed my identity with my clothes.

My mom had gotten me a new outfit for Easter that came with a top coat and hat. The new clothes were restrictive. I looked like a sissy in church the one time I wore them, but they were just the right style for a secret agent to dress in. I tried to be discreet and move around the ranch without drawing much attention to myself. This was difficult. When people see a young boy in a fedora sneaking through the pasture carrying a huge black suit case and talking to his shirt, they get suspicious. I looked the part, but had some restrictions due to lack of homeland cooperation.

I wanted great hair like all the secret agents on television had. Big hair was big stuff in those days. You could be the dorkiest loser in school, but if you had a lot of hair you got by.

My dad believed in getting his money's worth in everything, so when I got hair-cuts I came out with blaring white sidewalls and a crew cut. Our local barber was known to us as "Al the Butcher" and we tallied his victims daily. We would be standing around the school yard before the morning classes and discuss the grim statistics of the latest "buzz-cut" victims.

The early chitchat on the playground included the latest casualties. Someone in the know would be saying, "I heard Al got both the Harris boys last night. My sister was going by there and heard the screaming and yelling. I guess he took Jared down first. He cried like a baby. Then she said Mitchie begged for mercy right till the end, but Al scalped him, too."

I remember my own trips to Al and he was crafty. He'd give you a big warm smile and ask you how you wanted it.

"Just a little off the sides, please. Only a little trim. It's still pretty cold, and Dad said I could leave it kinda' long - really."

Al would nod his head in understanding and then adjust the setting on his clippers all the way down to "skinhead".

Afterward my hair was almost non-existent and definitely un-spy like. I looked like a candidate for the Bosley Method. I decided that one skill necessary to be a good spy is the ability to change your appearance. So before school the next morning I stood in front of the bathroom mirror and started working over the white sidewalls with black shoe polish. The right side turned out pretty good but I could never get the left side tolerable. It looked like someone smeared my head with axle grease. I sat at the breakfast table sideways with my good side leading. Dad was busy reading the paper and Mom was at the stove. My sister was on my left. I was hurrying through breakfast and just finished my toast.

"SKIP, WHAT IS THAT ALL OVER YOUR HEAD?" she asked.

"*Nothing,*" I said.

"THERE IS, TOO. THERE'S SOMETHING BLACK ALL OVER ON YOUR HEAD."

"No, there's not," I said.

I was now the center of attention, Dad put the paper down, and everyone darn sure wanted to take a good look at my head. Neither the left or the right side passed scrutiny. Most of the neighbors and my family knew how important spying was to me. They even contributed to my missions by giving me spy gifts, but my favorite was given the year of my hair episode.

I got a Secret Sam kit for my birthday that same year. It had a spring-loaded gun that shot darts and would adapt to shoot a big weighted projectile with a cap in it that would detonate on impact. There was a secret plastic knife hidden in the side, a decoder graph included, and the whole thing was pretty cool. All of my Secret Sam kit came in handy at one time or another during my missions, especially the gun.

I happened to see my sister riding an old buckskin ranch horse bareback down the county road one day - before she saw me. I immediately dropped down in the weeds for cover. My training convinced me that this was a job for the grenade launcher accessory in my arsenal. I loaded my Secret Sam gun and my timing was perfect. The bomb arced beautifully and popped on the road right in front of our old horse, Bucky. He was evidently aware of the dangers associated with grenade launchers because he swapped ends and quit the country. My sister was sitting on the road where Bucky had been.

I think I saw steam coming out of her ears. Did I mention my sister was bigger than me in those days? She could have torn me limb from limb. She just sat there on the gravel road until she got her wind back and then had me help catch her horse. She didn't even tell our folks. Corporal punishment was still viewed as acceptable behavior in those days and I would certainly have gotten a dose if she had told her story. That really bothered me - the fact that I could have gotten a whipping. I decided then that the spy business was too cruel for my sensitive nature.

Bruce came to our ranch that year as a favor to his father, the Reverend Herbert Harptone. Bruce was seventeen, unappreciative, and continually getting in trouble in town. This was bad for church business. He was the first person I ever saw with tape holding his glasses together and he reeked of bad cologne. Brill Cream was still in style and his hair gleamed with it. He had a bad complexion and he wore his father's old work clothes which hung on his wiry frame. The arrangement with his folks was, they were rid of him for the summer, and we could work him for slave wages. They got the better end of the deal.

"He reminds me of a coyote that's been shot at twice," Dad said to Mom that evening.

"His eyes bug out, and he keeps looking around behind himself."

"What will you do with him?" Mom asked. "I doubt he knows how to do much and I really would rather he didn't stay in the house."

"He can help you in the yard, and then we'll start him out picking rocks up on the butte top of the state land bench. He can sleep in the bunkhouse," Dad convinced Mom.

Bruce snooped around in drawers and peeked in windows.

In his patrol of the brush behind the bunk house, he became the first victim of one of my wild animal traps.

"It whipped my feet right out from under me and I had to cut myself down. Who set that trap?" he asked.

As much as I would have liked to take credit for the successful capture, I wanted to avoid getting beat up even more.

"Trap? What trap?" I asked. "Oh, the last hired man might have set it," I explained. "He said big pack rats kept crawling down the chimney of the bunk house, and it was waking him up at night. Maybe he was trying to thin them out."

"Big pack rats?" He questioned. "Around here?"

He started scratching himself as if he were fighting off fleas.

"Ya," I said. "I saw one so big he could stand on his hind legs and look right in the window there." I pointed to the bunkhouse.

I noticed Bruce started sleeping with the lights on. The next week Bruce and I were weeding my mother's garden and he asked me, "Are there many coyotes' around here? I think I hear them at night sometimes."

I enjoyed being an authority on something. I gave him a serious look and said, "Could be. It might also be the crazy widow Maki."

"Who's she?" He asked and started to scratch again.

"Well, Dad said my grandpa bought this place from a nutso lady named Maki. Her little boy got lost on this creek bottom and they never found him. You can still hear her ghost," I said.

"Her ghost? Really?" He said.

"Really. The lost boy's name was Howie and I guess some people still hear her calling for him. Howie—Howwieee-How – How –Howieeeee," I said solemnly.

I noticed Bruce started sleeping with the radio on, too.

Bruce's next job was to fill the loader bucket on the front end of our Massey Ferguson tractor with rocks. He was to pick them by hand from the middle of the field and then go dump the load on the side. He had strict instructions not to get too close to the edge of the high butte that the field was on top of. He took the second load of rocks right over to the steep edge to dump them so he could watch them roll down the hill. When he stopped suddenly at the brink of the hill, the weight of all the rocks in the front end caused the back wheels to come off the ground. Those wheels held the only brakes on the tractor. Down the hill he went - freewheeling. From the top to the bottom was about six hundred feet. We saw three huge divots where the two large rear tractor tires hit the ground and bounced with the brakes locked. It tore up huge chunks of sod. He hit a quaking aspen tree at the bottom that was about twelve inches around and bent it over. The tractor had enough momentum to move about twenty feet up the now slanted tree and then the big aspen sprung back up. All the branches held the tractor in place and it ended up that we had a tractor about ten feet up in a tree.

My dad was incredulous and inquired, "Didn't it scare you when you hit the barbed wire fence?"

"Fence?" he asked scratching his head. We weren't bored with Bruce around, and my sister Caren and I enjoyed our own adventures at Bruce's expense.

My sister and I were great cat trappers. There were lots of wild snarling cats on our place. They always showed up when we milked the cow looking for a handout. Caren and I had caught most of them and kept them in a huge cardboard box that the washing machine came in. For the cat trap we used an old mail box and put food inside. Then we hid in the bushes and pulled the lid shut with a long piece of string. We were too scared to open the big box or look inside because there were twelve pissed-off insane cats in there. We would feed them through a small hole and the yowling, hissing and clawing that took place inside of that box shook the ground.

It gave us the shivers. We knew we possessed a powerful entity with that box of contained frantic energy. Something like our own nuclear reactor or personal W.M.D.

I needed my hatchet to set up some more snares behind the bunk house, and I remembered I had left it in the wood box in the shop. I had crawled in the empty box to retrieve it and I saw Bruce coming. I thought it would be fun to hide from him so I shut the lid and peeked out through a knothole. Bruce was snooping again. He was looking in the glove boxes of the vehicles, going through bins, and rummaging under the work benches.

"Bruooose- - Ohh Brooooose," I called in my best quavering scary voice.

His head snapped around and he was certainly now on high alert. He looked briefly around for the source of the voice and then remembered he was itching. He continued his searching around the shop with less enthusiasm.

"Howie—Howwiee -- Howwiieee."

Bruce left the building at a brisk walk, without looking back and then he started running when he was clear of the door.

There was one huge gray tom that we couldn't catch. He was the last wild cat on the place that we knew of. We were kinda' scared of that big tom and we had named him the wolf cat. I had an old stinky trout that I had left in my fishing creel and I used it to bait the trap one day.

I didn't have to wait long until he went in that mail box like a gopher down his hole. I was beside myself with excitement. I had finally outwitted and captured the famous wolf cat of the Rim Rock Ranch. The grand slam trophy of wild cats. We had an old welding glove we used to get a hold of our prey and I put it on and cracked the lid to retrieve my prize. That cat saw daylight and rushed the exit. I tried to stop him. He bit down through the glove, and my thumbnail and wouldn't turn loose. I started howling like a lonely coyote and ran for the house with that huge cat hanging steadfast on my thumb. Dad heard my great wailing and came out to rescue me. After he pried that big tom off my hand, he asked, "How did you catch that cat, and what were you going to do with him?"

I told the whole story. How we had a whole big washing machine box full of wild cats, and that my sister was in on the deal.

"It was mostly her idea. I was just going along with her since she's older and bigger than me, and pretty much in charge."

"Get rid of em,'" he said. "Turn them all loose before you guys get hurt again."

Well, my sister and I had gone through a lot of work and cat food to trap those cats, and we weren't too anxious to just let them go on their own recognizance.

"…We could keep them in somewhere and tame them down," she said.

"Ya," I said. "I know just the spot."

This happened to be a day when my dad had farmed Bruce out to the neighbor who was stacking hay. Bruce got home late that night after a long hot day of handling bales. My sister and I intended to stay up to tell him that we were using the bunk house as a temporary-holding facility for our cats, but we forgot.

Dad had called Bruce's folks the next morning when he wasn't there for breakfast. He learned that Bruce had walked all the way to town overnight.

"That kid's a strange one," Dad said. "His folks seem pleased as punch though. His dad said he's *'a whole new boy and seems genuinely glad to be home. Outright grateful and really seems to appreciate us now.'* His dad told me, *'Thank you for helping us with our son. He had strayed from the path, but now he is found . The prodigal son has returned.'* Those were his exact words."

Dad pointed to the bunk house and asked, "Do you know it looks like that goofy kid jumped through the screen door last night instead of opening it?"

"Well, I'll be," Mom said, "You know I thought I heard something about ten-thirty, but I thought it was just one of the hogs stuck under a gate."

Proverbs 22:6

Dear Skip

Some of my readers often write in with questions and I would like to use this chapter to answer these inquiries. I would also like to clear up a misprint from an article I wrote that was carried in several livestock publications on medicating range bulls out in the pasture. An alert reader informed me of this oversight and I want to immediately clear up the issue. I sincerely apologize for any inconvenience, frustration or life-threatening injuries this might have caused.

In my article **"Pasture Doctoring for Dummies"** there is an error in the fifth paragraph describing the treatment method of using powerful antibiotics to heal the badly infected foot of a large herd bull. The seventh line should read –

Inject the hoof- rot shot to correct him.
Not – and this is of paramount importance -

Inject hot shot at rectum.

Dear Skip,

You told some pretty rough stories about your wife in the last book. Is she really like that?

Signed,
Dr. Phil

Dear Dr. Phil,

Actually I wandered from the truth somewhat in those previous stories. In fact, my spouse is lots meaner than I let on. I kept a lot of the really bad stuff out because I was concerned that I might give some of my young readers nightmares.

Dear Skip,

In a lot of the classic cowboy movies, they take a lot of time for singing and yodeling. How did that tradition originate?

Signed,
Slim Whitman

Dear Slim,

When a cowboy lassos something, he has to take a couple quick turns with the end of the lariat around the saddle horn. This is called "taking a dally." It is what holds the captured critter and restrains his progress. There is a hard knot on the end of this rope that whips around there at an extreme velocity if you loose your grip on it. As you know, the saddle horn is right in front of "Little Jimmy and the twins" while you are seated in the proper riding posture. The knot can snap a guy in that very sensitive area with a blinding impact. Hence the first yodel was born when the cowboy redirected his cries of pain into something like a song so his co-workers wouldn't tease him while he was checking himself out for damages and ooh whooing.

"Boy, I'll bet that really hurt when the rope slapped you right there in the gems –huh Slim?"

"Oh noo - oouwhoouhoo. There's still twoouwho-ouoo."

Another little factoid is that this is also how we discovered that an extremely high and sustained quavering voice is capable of shattering glass.

Dear Skip,

I hear a lot in the horse world lately about imprinting and what a good deal it is. What are your thoughts?

Signed,   Mimi from Meeteetse

Dear Mimi,

You know how a dentist has you do an imprint to get a crown or new dentures? You bite down on some clay so they can make a mold. Imagine you are the clay. I have permanent imprints from several of the horses I've known and I never did see the benefit. I also have an imprint of a number two horseshoe from a mare that kicked me.

Dear Skip,

My horse bucked me off. My dad told me to *get right back on and show him whose boss*, so I did. He bucked me off again. What do you think?

Signed,
Ella from Ekalaka

Dear Ella,

I think your horse is the C.E.O. and you're a slow learner.

Dear Skip,

I see a lot of newspaper advertisements listing different horses for sale, but some of the terminology has me confused. For instance what does "Green broke" refer to?
Signed,
Baffled in Bozeman

Dear Baffled,
In order to save space and time I will include a small glossary of excerpts of horse trader slang that is often found in newspaper advertisements. Green broke is basically the same thing as saying, "The gelding has thirty days riding."

This usually means the horse has been penned up for a couple of weeks and you don't always have to rope him to get him caught or tie him down to get the saddle on.

I will try to help with the interpretation of some of the terms that are commonly used when horses are traded.

Just say you see this snippet in an ad:
"Fifteen-year old mare- Arab and Rhodesian ridgeback cross - for experienced riders only."

If you have had the experience of qualifying for the N.F.R. in the saddle-bronc riding event, this horse might work out for you.

Or "Out of Moon Hancock and is real cowy."

The horse eats meat. Do not turn your back or get in the same corral with this animal.

An ad stating:
"This little filly has a lot of bottom."

This particular ad is in the wrong classification and should be moved over to the personals or dating section of the paper.

I once went to look at a four-year-old gelding that was advertised as a "kid's horse." He was a big red roan with a kind eye and he seemed quiet. I was thinking of buying him for Holly.

"My wife is pretty handy but she's no bronc rider," I said. "Does this horse buck?"

"This horse has never bucked with me," he said. "He is a bit fresh when you first start out is all. When I started him, he crow hopped a little but nothin' worth mentioning."

The guy was pretty fat and old. I figured if he rode him the horse had to be pretty gentle. The horse sure looked tame and he was a steal if he was broke at all. I knew what the canner price was. I figured the gelding weighed about a thousand pounds and did the math at the current price of forty cents per pound. I didn't want to insult the guy so I bid five hundred dollars.

"Sold." he said "but I can't take a check. My boss, the little woman, won't let me."

"I've got the cash," I said. "But do you mind if I ride him before I take him home to my wife. It's her birthday and I want to surprise her."

"I um - don't have a saddle here," he said as he grabbed the cash out of my hand.

"I do. I'll go get it," I said.

The fellow seemed a little nervous when I went to get on and started looking toward his car.

"I always found it helpful to lean way back if a horse ever bucked on me, and it never hurts to keep your chin tucked," he said.

I slowed down my saddling process and said, "I thought you said this horse only crow hopped a little."

"And I told you I didn't want to mention it. Now really dig in with your spurs and try to get some good holds with your feet if he gets a little nasty, and don't be too proud to pull leather if he sunfishes. You're not scared of him, are ya?" He said.

"The ad said he was a kid's horse," I said.

"Well, he was my kid's horse, now he's your wife's horse. My kid never got him rode though, and I never tried him. When I was young I used to be able to stick to em' like a cockle burr, but I'm getting a little long in the tooth now."

I looked to see if my money was still in sight. It sounded worse as he went on.

"I always thought if Junior would have tried harder to arch his chest and keep his toes turned out he coulda' got by that terrible third jump he throws. You might mention that to your wife. The little lady I'm married to made me put him up for sale after that last trip to the E.R."

I was breaking horses for a barn outside of Great Falls and another trainer brought a horse back that he started for the same outfit. He said the colt was "just too goofy."

The gelding was only two, and the other trainer said he had to hobble him and tied up a foot just to get a saddle on. I didn't think a two-year old should be that bad, so I took him over. I ended up liking the colt so much that I bought him. I called him Silver. He never did buck but he was always pretty lively. Even though he was a little fractious, he was beautiful to look at and he kept a light mouth the whole time. I owned him about three years and thought he would sell well at an upcoming cataloged horse sale.

It was an outside auction and we got to show our horses during the bidding in an arena. The horse sold for what I wanted and the guy who bought him came up to talk to me after the sale. I knew right away it was a bad fit. The buyer was an older guy with a big belly who was loud and really gruff acting. He even talked like McGruff, the crime dog. I told him about Silver's history and showed him the bit I used. I knew a friend who really wanted the horse, too, so I told him.

"If this horse doesn't work out for you, let me know. I will give your money back. A friend of mine wants him if you don't."

I gave him my phone number and three days later I got a call.

"Is that offer to buy back the horse still good?" he asked.

"Yes, what's wrong?" I asked.

"Nothing really," He said. "I think he is just too much horse for me."

"My friend still wants him so bring him in. I'll give your money back. It's no problem," I said.

I met the fellow and gave all his money back. He seemed happy and healthy and he even bought me a beer afterward.

He told me, "When I went to get on him I was a little nervous so I really cheeked him up. He started spinning like a top so I just got off. Then I called you. Like I said I think he is just a little too much horse for me at my age."

I don't think he expected me to be so willing to square up. He bought me a beer and even had me keep the halter that Silver was wearing. My friend that was interested took the horse and they got along well. He still owns him today.

I saw Mr. Big Belly five years later at a friend's wedding. I thought we had parted on good terms so I went up to visit with him.

"How are you?" I inquired.

"Not so good," He was glowering at me now. "I'm still having trouble with my shoulder from when that horse of yours banged me up."

I had never heard this story. It seemed like the fellow had been drinking, so I just tried to change the subject and left him alone.

Six years after that I saw the guy again at a funeral. I happened to be sitting across the same folding table as him at the wake afterwards. He was drinking lots of the keg beer. I didn't know if he would even remember me. I hoped not.

"How is it going?" I said.

"Terrible!" he said. "That damned horse you sold me left me with some aches and pains I have to live with every damned day!"

I did not want to debate this in front of all the people there, so I let it go again.

I couldn't help wondering why he seemed fine when he brought the horse back, and why the story had changed. I also really liked that horse and had started to feel pretty defensive.

My three kids all play the fiddle very well. They are asked to perform a lot and as a community service they used to entertain at a retirement home. We were sitting at a table there, after the kids played, eating our lunch. I saw old grumpy across the room but avoided him like the plague. This is seventeen years after he bought the horse from me. We needed extra folding chairs for Holly's folks and her other relatives. They were stacked up by "you know who".

"Please go get some more chairs, Skip," Holly said, "This is the third time I've asked and we really need them."

Hell, I had to go. He was sitting right beside the chairs glaring at me.

"Hello," I said, "I just need to get a few chairs."

"I'm crippled. That's how I am." He shouted. "Every since you stuck me with that man killer of a horse, I've had hell. I went to feed him one day and he pawed me right off the top rail of the fence and then he tried to stomp me into the dirt."

"I just need some chairs for the family, and I'll be out of your hair," I said.

"By God, if I was ten years younger, I'd show you where the bear shit in the buckwheat." He shouted.

He was still loud even in his advanced years and he had everyone's attention. I decided I had about a gut full of this guy's lies and abuse. It had been festering for some time. I figured there was no time like the present to set the record straight.

"You were just fine when I gave you all your money back!" I yelled. "The guy who took him after you has gotten along good with him for seventeen years, so he can't be too bad. What was your problem, Tubby?"

Can you imagine how awful I looked? Here I was in front of the whole family losing my temper. The good part was that he knew I finally had enough of his B.S. and he settled down some.

I left with some chairs.

"Really cool, Skip," Holly said. "You get in a big fight in front of my folks and the kids, too. It looked for awhile like you were going to strangle him."

"Hey! He swung at me with that walker first," I said. "And I was just trying to untangle those oxygen tubes. Somehow they got wrapped tight around his neck."

Proverbs 16:32

Bingo

The ranch I grew up on was in West-central Montana where winter overstayed its welcome. I always felt like my dad was trying to run more cows than our little place should hold. We put up hay all summer and then fed hay from December to mid-May. There were only about six weeks we weren't handling those little square bales in one form or another so I got lots of practice stacking hay. The rest of the year we were either fencing or moving cattle around. We didn't have any good equipment. It was mostly cobbled together by welding rod, baling wire, and hope. We got in the habit of holding our breath all haying season. Help was cheap so we got along with what we had and made up in man hours what we lacked in machinery. Our place usually needed a repairman more than a cowboy so my dad hired guys like Ralph.

We hired Indians to help pick hay and anybody we could get for the rest of the work. The main criteria for being an employee on our ranch was to work long hours for next to nothing. The turnover of hired hands was a great source of education and entertainment for us kids. Once in awhile we met people walking back to town who had just quit while we were hauling the new workers home. Some of those guys didn't even ask for their last paycheck. They just left - sometimes with a couple of my grandma's chickens.

Most of the time they slept in our house somewhere, and my mom fed them and washed their clothes.

Since some of them lived with us, we got to know them pretty well. A few of them we knew much too well. My dad hired a guy named "Bud Long-Robes" to help dig ditches. When I was about eight years old, Bud Long-Robes gave me a gift, his switchblade knife with a bright orange handle. My mom exercised her right of confiscation.

Our usual cowboy crew was my dad, my sister and me, my Grandma Ruth from my dad's side, and our present hired man. We were pretty mechanical when it came to moving or working our cattle and I remember lots of hollering, barking, bawling, and profane adjectives. It seemed like we were at war with the cattle, and as I remember, the dogs were always standing in the gate we needed to go through.

Ralph worked for my dad off and on and he lived in town with my other grandma. I guess that made him my common-law grandpa. He wasn't really much like a grandfather either, but more like a naughty uncle who might give you some beer or offer you a smoke. Ralph had come from Missouri and had worked either as a bartender or mechanic all his life. He had an endless hoard of dirty jokes that made him cackle every time he repeated them. Most didn't make any sense to me, but I would usually muster up a weak laugh out of respect for his seniority. He was a good mechanic and I made sure we were friends when I was old enough to need his help working on my truck. His age was somewhere around sixty but his face and liver were much older. An accident in a tire shop years before had left an ugly pitted dent in his right temple, and he had the unsettling habit of scratching at it with a match stick after every meal. He had an interesting battle-scarred nose and bright eyes behind some thick filmy glasses. Ralph loved to talk, smoke Salem cigarettes, and play bingo at the Moose Hall in Great Falls. He filled a water glass with whiskey every night as soon as he was done working and put in a couple ice cubes to top it off.

A friend who was helping us out through a haying season asked him after some time about the generous amount of bourbon he allowed himself.

"The doctor wants me to only have one drink a day — so, by God, I make er' a good one," Ralph confessed.

"Aren't you worried that you might be hooked?" Our friend asked later that summer.

"Hell no!" Ralph said. "Cause I never intend to quit."

We seemed to schedule every Friday around his evening bingo game in town.

Our ranch held a forest service permit in the Highwood Mountains that allowed us to pasture a certain number of cattle in common with some other neighboring ranches. We had a community roundup every fall that I really enjoyed. There was always a campfire at the main corral, and usually some of other kids my age. The women would have warm food ready when we got back with cattle, and we would eat sitting on the damp leaves under the bright yellow quaking aspens. My dad let me carry a twenty-two pistol in my saddle pocket sometimes to shoot mountain grouse and if it was early we could spot elk on the high ridges. I loved riding my horse anyway, and it took a day or so to find all the cattle and then two days to trail them home. I missed some school because of all this "work" and that made it all the better.

One Friday shortly after the roundup Dad sent Ralph and me up to get a calf that we had missed. A neighbor, who was short some livestock, had spotted him when he was searching for some of his strays, and he told my dad where we should look. This was well before everyone had a gooseneck stock trailer so we loaded our horses in an old blue two-ton truck and set off.

"I sure hope this don't make me late for my bingo game tonight. I'm the caller and they won't know what to do without me," Ralph said.

Those old trucks weren't known for their speed or big engines so it took a long time to get up to the corrals, especially with Ralph's chain smoking and one-sided conversation.

"Ya know all I get for calling out the bingo numbers is free beer, so I drink all I can. Seems to me I ought to get a supper or some free drink tickets, too. I might just up and quit one-a-these days. That'll show 'em. They'd be up shit creek without me - I'll tell ya,- yessiree. You know how to make a hunderd' little old ladies swear? Just say bingo. Hee hee."

He took another long drag on his latest cigarette and went on.

"Did I ever mention that some of them old gals that show up can't even afford to eat decent but they buy five cards ever' game. That widow Larson is tight as a knat's ass stretched over a rain barrel when it comes to buyin' anything else, but she's got plenty to spend on bingo games. Ya know once I burnt my car up back in Saint Louis to collect the insurance money?" And so it went. I envied the horses their fresh air and isolation in the back of the truck.

When we finally got there, we backed the truck up to a big dirt bank so we could jump the horses out. The calf was right where he was supposed to be but was as wild as an elk. He looked like he had been bummed from his mom in the spring and so he was pot-bellied and rough-haired. The country was unfriendly for roping and he got away from us quite a few times. I tried to get him as close to the truck as we could before we roped him because I knew he wouldn't lead or drag too easily.

I would pull him awhile and he would choke down. We would let him up to get some air and repeat the process. It was taking quite awhile to get him halter broke, but we made progress and Ralph never quit talking or worrying over his impending bingo duties the whole time.

"You know I've never been late yet for my bingo game. Not one time. Your grandma will be a spittin' and battin' her eyes like a toad in a hail storm if I aint' there early to pick' er up. She'll have a shit-fit I'll tell ya'. By God, she's getting fat! Got jowls on er' anymore like a fattlin' hog. She likes to get there ahead of time so she can sort out the cards she likes. My third wife liked bingo, too. She left me and took all my money while I was in the hospital with this big gash on my head. Hey, did I ever tell ya how me and my cousin Scroggins blew up the outhouse with dynamite when we were in the third grade?" he said.

When we finally got the calf drug to the truck, Ralph opened the end gate and we got the calf wrestled in. After we took off the rope, that wild steer tried every way he could to crawl out or jump over the stock rack. Those old end gates were horrible. They grudgingly moved up and down on tracks that were usually bent or full of frozen mud. Someone with a sense of humor who had seen a French guillotine must have invented that gate system, and you could never seem to get them opened when you wanted or shut when you needed.

Our plan was for Ralph to hold up the gate while simultaneously keeping the calf spooked to the front of the truck. I was going to lead the horses in, one at a time under the gate. It was at the critical point of leading in the second horse when the calf made a determined charge at the gate and his freedom. Ralph threw both hands out in front of him and shouted,

"Whoa!"

The gate chose that moment to work perfectly and came crashing down on Ralph's head. He dropped quicker than the President's approval rating. The calf didn't get out, and he took out his frustration on Ralph's head which was pinched firmly under the mostly closed gate. When I got him out from under there, he was a mess. His noggin didn't look too good under the best of circumstances and now it was smeared with manure and calf snot to boot.

He was unconscious, but I wouldn't have done C.P.R. even if I would have known how. He was breathing so I figured I'd wait and see if he might come good on his own. After a little time, I thought I ought to try to do something. Besides, I needed him to drive the big truck home. I grabbed his wrists and started pumping his arms up and down to try to wake him up a little. The first promising sign of life was a low groan that turned into a *ba baa baa* sound. Then finally, "baa, bu, beeee, ---- bingo."

Proverbs 21:23

My Dad

My grandfather had a second grade education. He worked on ranches and later leased them to try to make a living. He trapped beaver and played the fiddle for country dances. He also started young and spoiled horses under a saddle or in a harness for extra money. My dad told me that whenever there was a really bad horse in our community they brought it to my grandpa. My grandmother and he had three sons –Ray, Gene, and my dad. My father attended eight different country schools in eight years because the places they leased kept getting sold. Grandpa bought a lot of property around the time of the Depression and the home place was where I grew up. There was always a mortgage hanging over our heads. I would have been the only son on a third generation cattle ranch had we kept it. If my folks could have held on to the place and turned it over to me, it would have come along with its own debts and other obligations. That is the way my dad got it and I don't think he wished that burden on me. My folks sold it when I was twenty-two, and I was quite unprepared and unwilling to do anything else.

My dad's name was Jake. He looked like a Jake. He had big shoulders and strong hands. Dad was barrel-chested, had a great smile, and blue twinkly eyes with huge puffy bags under them.

"I've got a fifth of scotch under each eye," he would say.

Dad didn't deny himself much. His two primary moods were wild exuberance and deep depression. He died right after his fifty-third birthday, and, in that short lifetime, he had exhausted almost all of his financial, physical, and emotional resources.

I think my dad didn't know what to do with me until I was old enough to fish, hunt, and work. Then we had a lot of fun. Both my folks were very good to me and loved me unconditionally. He never once spanked me and was quite tolerant of my impulsive and rambunctious nature. Dad always bragged me up. If my only achievement in life was to be the town drunk, he would have been sure that I was the best town drunk that ever spilled a beer.

I wrecked his Willy's jeep when I was only eight. He loved that jeep and kept it clean and in good shape. He had been giving me driving lessons the night before and after several trips into the ditch he decided "I was just too little to drive." I disagreed with the opinion.

Just because I couldn't see over the dash or reach the pedals didn't mean I couldn't drive. In fact, I had been driving for years if you count steering the feed truck around in circles in low gear while someone kicked hay off the back.

The morning milking job was mine. When Dad was up on the hill cutting hay, Mom, my sister, and my grandma were still asleep. For some reason, I decided I would just drive over to the corral to milk those cows that morning and save the walk. The corral was about a half a mile away, and I had to drive out on the county road and cross a bridge with no sides. That old jeep would start in first gear, so away I went. I got it out of the yard and out onto the road. I could not see over the dash and the jeep didn't have doors. I just watched out the side and when it seemed like I was getting too far from the other ditch, I turned back to the middle.

When it seemed like I was outta' road on my side, I steered the other way. I also had to turn off the road and down the lane to the corrals and hit the bridge just right. The bridge over the creek was pretty high. My best explanation for my survival that day is that I'm sure God was helping me steer, and, of course, he did a fine job.

When I got to the corral I remembered, with no small amount of panic, that in my lesson we had only gone over starting and steering—nothing about stopping. I hadn't even thought about that till right then and the issue was coming up in a hurry. I remember thinking, "By golly, the key turned her on - maybe the key can shut this thing down."

I had a little too much speed to stop in time. I managed to miss the railroad ties that were set as posts but there was no missing the poles. The windshield folded down on to the hood on those old jeeps and fortunately it was strapped down. We were just the right height to drive under the top two poles on three sections of the fence before the jeep coasted to a stop. I ended up well inside the sorting alley along with all the broken lumber I had plowed up with the grill guard.

I could see this was a problem, and I tried to figure out some way to put a positive spin on the deal while I was nervously milking my cows. There was no way Dad wouldn't find out, so I decided I would be the one to tell him. He was almost a mile away swathing hay and I walked up there. It would have been a perfect Montana July morning, except for the dread I felt in my stomach.

There was no wind and the fresh cut hay smelled great. It took about fifteen minutes to make a round in the hay field he was cutting. He saw me waiting at the gate and told me how pleased he was to have some company and how nice it was of me to come see him.

He had to yell over the roar of the engine. I didn't want to ruin this special father-son moment we had going, so I just rode around with him for a few rounds. Then I went a few more. If we could have cut hay forever in that field, it would have been fine with me. But, I knew I had to tell him eventually. That old hay swather didn't have a cab and it was really loud up there beside my dad.

"Dad, I wrecked the jeep," I said quietly.

He either didn't hear or understand what I said because he just smiled and nodded.

"Dad, I wrecked the jeep in the corrals," I said louder. He heard me that time and stopped the swather.

"You did what?" He said incredulously.

I told the whole story on the way back. I'm not sure he believed me until we got to where we could see the jeep sitting under a pile of poles well inside the corrals. To me the jeep looked kind of naughty - like it might have driven over there on its own and caused all that trouble by itself. We stopped to examine the damage and got my full milk buckets. He didn't talk to me and it was a long ride back to the house.

I never did get in any trouble over that. I waited for a long time to see what he would do but nothing ever happened. I guess it scared us all enough that they just were relieved it worked out how it did. It went without saying that I was grounded from driving. Both of us kids were so far out in the country that we were pretty much grounded from everything anyway so it was no big deal. I took it upon myself to repair the corral and it took me most of the month. I went over there every night after dinner and pounded (more like tapped) on those big spikes with my puny arms to get the rails back in place.

I killed a cow with my rope when I was in high school. She was a good young bred cow. I was trying to get her across the road from a lot I was sorting out of. After a couple failed attempts to chase her over, I roped her and drug her. She didn't get up. I had broken her neck. My grandma and I butchered her and hung her in the shop. My dad was gone, and I knew I had done something that was very stupid and expensive. Even though my dad was constantly telling me to slow down and let the cattle find their own way, I usually went way too fast and pushed too hard. I always thought I was in a hurry and tore around on my horse like the Lone Ranger. It led to a lot of extra work, frustration, and fencing for all of us. I told my dad what I had done when he got home and showed him the cow like it was some sort of big game trophy. He just shook his head and sighed.

Then he told me, "At least you butchered her right away so the meat didn't go to waste."

I have two sons of my own that rope things. I would not have been so understanding.

The year after I graduated from high school we were kind of *even* for awhile and in my mind competitive. Dad asked me more and he ordered me less. He could still outshoot me and easily best me arm wrestling, but he let me think I came close. We were in financial trouble by then and my dad tended to deny big problems until they were insurmountable and then he dealt with the stress and strain by having a few boiler-makers. Creditors were calling, lawyers sent us registered mail, and there were hard times and sleepless nights. Losing a ranch is not a quick amputation of your hearth and home. It is more like a terminal illness of attrition in which your choices and well-being are devastated on a monthly basis.

We had sold our calves two different ways that fall and we were sorting pairs on a gray and windy October day.

Dad would point out a cow and her calf and it was my job to ease them out a gate. He rode this pokey old Appaloosa and that really irritated me. I usually rode a pretty lively horse and I figured he ought to as well.

We were quite a pair. That old appy moped along like he was on his last legs with his nose almost touching the ground and my horse that day was as wild as a buck deer.

I remember asking my dad, "Can that horse even go fast enough to scatter his own turds?"

"He's a lot better than that run-away you're ridin'," he said.

"At least I know he's not dead," I replied.

"It must be like trying to stop a train with a set of bridle reins," he said.

My dad knew stock and could really remember a cow. At that time, they all looked pretty much the same to me. I was taking a pair out on the other end of the big lot we were using. I hurried them too much and right at the gate the cow went through, but the calf cut back in with the noisy large herd we were working. Dad was focused on finding a cow and hadn't seen my failed attempt. I had to really keep my eye on that calf so he wouldn't get lost in the crowd of bawling cattle. I worked the calf into a corner, took a long throw and caught that big fall steer right around the belly. My horse didn't like it any better than the calf. I had used my whole rope, and we came barreling through the lot with my horse and the calf both bucking on each end. It was thirty feet of "the nylon jump rope from Hell." We were covering a lot of country fast and heading right toward the back of my dad and his oblivious horse.

If I had it to do it over, I would have un-dallied and saved my dad the pain.

That rope hit him right between the small of his back and the cantle of the saddle. He was taken completely by surprise, and it launched and lifted him into a sort-of reverse double gainer with a half twist. His height and form on this exercise were world class, but he really blew the landing. Dad had achieved a bit of a paunch by then and he hit hard. I still remember how he looked and the exasperated expression when we went ripping over him on through the cow lot. It was like, *What did I ever do to you?*

"Look out!" I yelled as we were bouncing by.

"Why? Are you coming back?" he gasped.

When I got my horse and the calf stopped, I yelled to him.

"Did that hurt you?"

"Well I don't think ya' done me a damn bit of good."

The sad fact is that I did so many ignorant things in those days that this latest escapade didn't even stand out much. Like the old adage—*you've got to be tough if you're gonna' be stupid*. Well, the people around you have to be tough, too, and my excessive zeal and shortsighted actions have caused a lot of scabs in my day. Unfortunately, not all of them were my own.

My dad's health really went downhill in those next few years and he just kinda' gave up. He had his first heart attack and I felt like he lived too hard for his own good. We sold the ranch and were going to move to town. I remember that I was self-absorbed on what would become of me and where I would fit in the world. I did not want to leave and put off packing until I had to.

My dad told me one morning, "You're either going to have to get moved out or hire on with the new owner - and I don't think you'd get along too well."

"At least it would be something I knew how to do and that I liked doing," I said.

"You can do anything you want. Go back to college. Take some time off."

"At least you had the chance to try at this," I said. "I never will. There's no way I'll ever have a ranch of my own."

He said, "You'll do just fine. You'll find something better than to spend your life worrying and sweating blood on some damned old thankless ranch."

"We don't even have a place for our horses or our dogs," I said.

"We'll find somewhere for the horses we don't sell and we will just put the dogs to sleep. It wouldn't be fair to them in town."

He lowered his voice a little and went on, "Everything was against me from the start. My neighbors made all that money in those good years I was away in the Army. I never had that chance, and it's the bankers in this country that decide who's gonna' make it and who isn't. They won't loan enough money to make this a profitable operation."

The guy who bought the place was pretty good about it and let us take our time moving out. Dad did not want to have an auction so we ended up moving a ranch full of equipment, gear, furniture, and junk into storage. I was at an age where I figured I knew about everything and my dad didn't know anything. Between that and the frustration and hopelessness of the loss of the family ranch, my dad and I didn't get along too well that year.

We had packed into the wilderness elk hunting almost every fall that I was old enough to hunt. I didn't want that tradition to end. I looked forward to those trips all year, and it was something to hang on to. Dad didn't think he was healthy enough to go. I thought he was and persuaded him.

My mom hates camping, but she is such a good sport and was concerned enough about Dad that she went along just so we wouldn't be alone. We took a bunch of extra food and gear because we wanted to make it a little nicer for Mom, and it ended up that we packed our stock too heavy. I wasn't too worried because it was only about nine miles to where we usually camped and it was a fairly easy trail. When we got to the spot we usually camped, someone was already there.

We were wore out and it was getting late in the day. Dad wanted to just camp somewhere close, but I wanted to go up on the mountain we were going to hunt and find a spot. That's what we did. We went till dark on a pretty rough trail and made a hurried camp on a gloomy little clearing. Dad was really tired.

My idea was to camp close to where we hunt, ready for the next morning. We did, but a snow storm had come in overnight and visibility was so poor that we couldn't see more than a hundred feet. We went out for awhile anyway but gave up after we kept getting turned around. It seemed like it would be best to move our camp to lower country and hopefully out of the storm.

After we got the horses packed, we started back down the mountain each leading two pack-horses. Dad was going first and riding that same appy I was so fond of. The trail was bad and it had lots of dead-fall. On a small hill, his horse had to jump a log across the trail; and instead of going right over, he danced around on his hind legs first.

The first pack horse had his head down and didn't stop for Dad's horse. He was muscling up the hill like a work horse because of his big load, and he hit Dad's horse from behind and knocked him off the trail. We had on our heavy coats and chaps because of the weather, and so ended up pretty encumbered. Dad tried to get off the uphill side while his horse was falling but didn't make it, and the horse landed on a tree with my dad's leg in between. His horse got up and limped off but Dad laid there.

His leg was broken badly. I helped him so he could sit up against a tree. He knew his leg was broken because he heard it snap.

After we talked about his broken leg, he wanted me to ride out to get help. I did not like that idea at all. It would be dark before I got out. There was nowhere to land a helicopter even if we could find him in the snow storm. He was wet and cold. Of course, I was concerned about his heart. Even with Mom staying there, I couldn't leave him. I believed that if I did, he would probably be dead by the time I got back. I was determined to get him on a horse and to safety.

Think about getting on a horse with one leg. You can't do it. You need a leg to stand on and a leg to put in the stirrup. His appy was the only really gentle horse we had along and now he was too lame to do us any good. As usual I was riding a colt, and when I led him over by Dad, he shied and snorted. I had four broken ribs from a rodeo injury the month before so I wasn't at my best either. To make matters even worse my dad out-weighed me by seventy pounds. I could pick him up but I was too short to get him high enough. I tried to get him up on my horse, but the horse kept shying away and I just couldn't lift him high enough for his good leg to hit the stirrup. Mom tried to hold the horse in one place and I tried mightily two times to get him on. You can imagine how painful those failed attempts were for my dad. Both times he told me to just leave him and go get help.

In the years since, I have told my wife about most of the wild antics and escapades of my youth. We fellows who act first and think later achieve some pretty exciting experiences and colorful stories along with our scars, gimps, and arthritis.

She once asked me, "When did you start getting smarter? I mean at what point in your life did you start wising up a little?"

Well, I can tell you I grew up about twenty years in ten minutes on the mountain that day.

It came to me that, at every step, I was completely responsible for this impossible predicament. I was about to lose my dad and the best friend I ever had on this earth, and it was one hundred percent my fault.

I talked him into trying one more time. I found a perfect setup just downhill from us. Three young trees grew in about a five-foot triangle on a side hill. I led my colt up to one tree and tied him as short as I could and between the two other trees. I let the uphill stirrup down all the way, pulled my dad over there and splinted his leg. I had him stand up and lean against a tree, and then I got on my hands and knees and had him straddle my neck. The horse couldn't move away because of the downhill tree beside him, and I was able to stand up enough for him to get the stirrup with his good leg. I left all the other stock right there and led him off the mountain with Mom following. In about ten throbbing hours, my dad was alive and in the emergency room of the Great Falls hospital.

Dad lived about four more years after that. He never met any of my kids or saw many of my successes. Although he had a truck- load of issues and I disagreed with many of his choices, I still miss him every day. Because, of course, I didn't love him because of what he did or who he was.

I loved him because he was my dad.

Proverbs 23:22

Fist Fightin'

I'm no warrior when it comes to fisticuffs. Some kids have great stories about their dad disarming a mugger or punching out a bully. My kids know stories about some of my old battles, but they would rather I'd not repeat them.

I'm not easily offended. I have figured out that if someone doesn't like me, becoming angry or violent in response to their opinion is optional. Most of the time when someone makes a disparaging remark regarding my behavior or attributes, it's accurate so there is usually no big issue to defend.

When the necessity came for a physical confrontation, it was always because I was trying to defend or rescue some friend or relative in immediate peril. I got along pretty good with everyone in grade and high school so my first experience in fist fighting came along with my college education. I went to Montana State University or "Moo-U." This was not because of the accreditation or location, but because they had the best rodeo team; and when I was eighteen, pretty much all I cared about was rodeo and girls.

This all happened quite awhile ago and was before the "five- year rule," which basically states your eligibility for college rodeo ends five years after you graduate from high school.

There were guys on our team in their late twenties and thirties who went to the NFR and were only in college because it was a lot easier and more fun than feeding cows on their dad's ranch.

Of course, those same guys had all the women, buckles, and money.

My other freshmen buddies and I were so shy and ranchie that we could hardly take a long look at a girl without blushing. There was no way we would risk talking to a girl we didn't know, and we were quite fascinated and confused by their behavior. We always hoped and figured some country-type cowgirls might just naturally gravitate toward rough-stock riders and take some of the risk out of the deal.

Our logic was that a pretty girl sees a guy with very limited vocabulary or disposable income who mechanically straps his hand to an enraged bull. Pretty girl thinks, *"Wow, I want to initiate a conversation with that guy that will ultimately lead to romance."* If you have ever seen a bunch of yearling steers ganged up in a corner watching the bulls over the fence into the cow pasture, you have some idea of our plight. We were pretty sure there was something interesting and exciting going on over there; we just couldn't put our finger on it.

I can see now that our train of logic was a couple boxcars short. We were mostly hung-over, brain-rattled misfits, and our personal development had pretty much ended once we shaped our cowboy hats. It took me a long time to figure out that while we were pounding all around the country competing in rodeos, the hometown boys were rounding up all the decent girls. At the end of the day, the only females we made lasting relationships with were some unsympathetic nurses.

There were four of us freshmen who competed on the college rodeo team and most of the other team members avoided us.

It seemed like they were worried that our nerdiness might be contagious. We had to travel to the rodeos together, usually four of us in the front seat of a truck. When we hung out at the Student Union Building on campus where the more successful and studly rodeo team members gathered, we sat at our own table. One highlight in our social lives was the weekly rodeo club meetings where we would discuss practice and the upcoming spring rodeo. We always went to the same bar afterwards and drank pitchers of beer together. Once a year we would have a rodeo club dance open only to the members and their dates. Everyone who was anyone would be there.

My best buddy Allen and I wanted to go, but fat chance if we'd ever line up dates. Our previous futile attempts at conversing with the available girls had involved stuttering and drinking lots of beer. The alcohol was a necessary prerequisite so we could work up enough courage to subject them to some rehearsed line. We were not too articulate in the best of settings and between all the beer and our jumpy nerves we could barely slobber out our intentions or names. The other big problems we had were that our window of opportunity for conversation was pretty short and our level of judgment proved out to be terrible. First we were too shy, then there were a couple of minutes where we would try to hook up; and right after that, we were so wild no one but a bouncer would have anything to do with us. So, unless there happened to be a girl handy at the perfect time, we were out of luck. We always tried to get a table by the girls' bathroom so we could get a couple tries at em' coming and going, but our success still remained limited. Allen had a fairly new car we would use to cruise for chicks. He kept it really nice and was always cleaning and waxing it.

There were a couple old gals who wanted to use us to get into the dance. They used all their charm to get our attention, batting their eyes and waving at us from the bar.

The place was smoky and it turned out they were fighting flies. Anyway, when Allen went to light their cigars, Melba said, "Connie and I want to go to the rodeo dance, and we'll let you boys take us if you don't try any funny stuff. No smoochin' or grabbin' unless we're doin' it. And you guys buy the drinks."

She wasn't a real smooth talker and had a cloudy reputation. We also guessed they might have very little to do with us once we got there. All our hard work and late-night reconnaissance had finally paid off.

I had a lot to do to get ready. This was going to take some money and planning. Ladies like these were probably used to fancy food and high living. We could take Allen's car, and it was just luck that dinner was provided because the girls looked like big eaters. I needed some new clothes, a haircut and some snappy banter ready for the evening conversation. We both got our hair cut at the beauty school downtown. You had to put up with a few nicks and cuts, but the price was right and we needed all our extra money for entry fees and beer. Allen was pretty shaggy and awfully head shy about clippers in the hands of the nervous students. I guess his dad used to cut his hair and besides being shaky, he used the same set of shears trimming Allen's hair that he used for the dogs and horses. Allen always claimed they jerked out as much as they cut; and when he left home, he quit getting haircuts. I thought for awhile we would have to use a foot rope or bite his ear to get him to hold still enough to get the grooming process complete.

Dressing up had always been easy before. We would wear our bluest Wranglers and least wrinkly shirt. If you look back to pictures from the seventies, you can see we were not afraid to take a fashion risk now and again.

Polyester with loud patterns was in style so I bought a new shirt that Elvis would have been proud of and a fancy pair of jeans with a houndstooth design from the good store, Hoglunds Western Wear, up in Great Falls. I looked good.

We picked up the girls right on time and they both got in the back seat. Like I say, I was kind of new at this dating stuff so I didn't worry about it but hoped the situation would change by the time we drove home. My head was swimming with the satisfaction of landing dates for the big event and we were plenty thirsty so a lot of the night was a blur. I do barely remember trying to waltz through a two-step and I polkaed through a jitter bug with Allen trying to lead. We were having so much fun that we lost track of the girls until it was time to close the bar. A friend told us about a party and bonfire down by the river. It sure seemed like that would be our best chance for some attention from these hot babes we were travelin' with.

There ended up being two fires down there and they were a little ways apart. Allen and I ended up at a fire with a couple of loggers. The girls and the rest of the rodeo crowd were at the other one. I was somewhat zoned out watching the fire and I remember Allen was giving one of the loggers a hard time. The next thing I remembered was seeing Allen on his back with the logger on top of him. He was using Allen's head for a punching bag. It was obvious Allen needed some relief so I ran in and got my arm around the logger's neck to get him choked down a bit. The guy put up quite a tussle, but I got Allen loose. The flaw in my plan was that the logger had a friend, too. He grabbed me from behind in a big bear hug and picked me clear off the ground. The guy was about the same size as a dump truck. I was kicking and squirming for all I was worth and calling him every name in the book. This fellow just squeezed a little tighter and calmly said, "Now, settle down, Sonny, and no one will get hurt."

I had a different idea, and I finally managed to get my leg tangled up in his enough to get him tripped down to the ground. Luckily, the fellow was kind enough to make sure he didn't land on me or you wouldn't be reading this story today. We rolled around in focused combat right through the flames. My new Lee check jeans turned out to be highly flammable. I quit wrestling right then and went to fighting fire. I was trying to put my pants out and the big logger was helping me. The girls had heard my war cry, which they later described as *"somebody screaming like a little girl."* They came to the rescue about the time our battle was over. All the fight was out of Allen, and as for me, I found it impossible to keep bad feelings against someone who just helped put out the fire progressing up my legs. I felt more like hugging him than punching him, so I guessed our work there was done.

It was a long ride home. The girls were both in the front with us in the back this time. I estimated there was very little chance for romance. Allen's eyes were both swollen shut and he was in a pretty glum mood. I was about medium rare. The girls weren't talking at all and seemed to be in a hurry to get home. I could sense our relationship was in transition. I was trying to cheer Allen up to ease the tension a little, but the only thing he asked was, "Who's smoking in my car?"

So I told him, "It's just my pants."

2 Timothy 4:7

Dances with Hooves

"I don't know how excited Boyd is going to be about me bringing you up here. He likes to work alone. We worry about him way up here by himself -- and he's worked for our family for so long that we feel like he's part of it."

My boss, Errol Galt, whose family owned the sprawling 71 Ranch, was delivering me to a cow camp on the west slope of the Crazy Mountains. I had offered to take my own pick-up, but he said I'd never find the place. We were driving through the big clean country east of Ringling, Montana, and had been traveling on ranch property for almost an hour already. I was supposed to stay and help an old cowboy named Boyd Anderson, a legend in these parts. I wasn't too worried about his reputation for being sullen and cranky. I could usually get most people to warm up to me quite quickly and usually even become friends. Actually, he sounded like an excellent companion to me, with a great life-style. He rode horses all day in beautiful country. He lived in a remote cabin with no responsibilities other than his cows and, in general, answered to no one. Other than the fact that by age thirty-six he had spent half of his life in prison, he sounded like an excellent role model for an up-and-coming young cowboy like me.

The cow-camp was great. The late evening light brightened an old log barn and cabin set in a quaking aspen meadow complete with a hitching rail and some pens. Various white shed elk horns and grazing horses decorated the scene. I fell in love with the place at once.

Boyd was out chopping kindling when we drove in. This seemed appropriate because he looked like an ax murderer anyway. I was hoping to meet someone like Charlie Russell. He looked more like Charlie Manson.

"I brought you up some grub and fencing supplies and a little help," Errol offered. "See if you can teach him how to handle cattle and help him get the lay of the land."

Boyd looked up from his chopping block through his stringy black hair and grunted with disgust. 'No one told me he was an Indian,' I thought, as we unloaded the last of my gear. It sure seemed like Errol hurried to get out of there. It felt more like Boyd was Errol's boss than the other way around. You might have just as well asked Hillary Clinton if Monica could come to her house to stay for a few days. I wished again mightily that I had my own truck as a means of escape.

"There's some penicillin and other vet supplies in the cardboard box so you better put 'em in your fridge. We contracted 400 steers to Tommy Lane so try to have about 450 steer pairs in the Haypress pasture by the first of October. Don't bring any more than that. We don't want to give Tommy too many to sort through, " Errol said, as he got into his pickup. I could tell he was trying to lighten the mood a little, but it wasn't working.

Errol and my enthusiasm left simultaneously.

I felt like a bastard calf at a roundup.

If I had any hopes of a friendly greeting or a "Cowboy Orientation" event, they were quickly dashed. Without a word, Boyd grabbed up some wood, went to his cabin, and shut the door.

Shit, this is going to be a long summer. I unrolled my bed on an old saggy wire cot in the cabin where Errol put my stuff. Since we didn't know about the dangers of Hantavirus or Giardia in those days, we were reasonably safe from those diseases. There were, however, plenty of mice to keep me company as I fretted and turned all night. I woke up once to see a rodent in the doorway of my cabin approximately the size of a beaver. I learned later that I shared my room with a musky groundhog. I didn't know what else to do so I prayed he was not carnivorous and hid under my blankets.

The next thing I heard, Boyd rode his horse by my cabin in the very early morning, presumably leaving for his day's work on the range. I was getting pretty damn hungry, but I didn't want to go into his cabin and dig around for food. I just went down to the pen to try to catch a horse and get going as soon as I could. I intended to impress Boyd with my skills as a cowboy and good hard work.

Three horses grazed there – all shod. An older looking fat bay gelding with saddle marks walked up to me, so I took him. I could hear quite a bunch of cattle bawling way off so I figured that's where Boyd was working. Almost a mile from the cabin, on the trail I followed, I came to a salt-ground. This horse acted awfully nervous about this damn salt-ground so I tried to gently and quietly guide him through. Well, he could buck pretty good for a fat old horse and he also spun to the left. He flopped me off on my belly, and I left a track across a fresh cow pie with my right forearm. I peeked up over the sagebrush, like a gopher, to see if Boyd had seen my failed bronc ride.

Thankfully he was nowhere in sight. I took off walkin' back to the cow camp where I found my horse waiting for me. He looked like he was joking with the other horses over the fence. They seemed to be having a great time and I thought I overheard something about an alaman-left at the salt-ground and then a big horselaugh.

Well, I got on him again and when we got to that same salt-ground, I took a really deep seat and a good hold on the reins. This time he sucked back and turned hard to the right. The only difference in results was that I landed about two feet over to the side of the cowpie I had left the track in. I think he tried to plant me in the same one, and then he loped back to his buddies at the barn to tell them what a slow learner I was. I had gotten to know the country pretty good between that particular salt-ground and the cabin so I didn't see any need to ride back quite the same way after I caught the horse again. It sure seemed like it might be a long summer.

It was obviously very late by the time I caught up with Boyd and all his cattle. He was gathering pairs out of some smaller side drainages and throwing them together on the bottom of a big valley. He had about four or five hundred pairs so far—just him and his dog. It seemed like he was trying to move the whole herd north so I guessed he must be changing pastures. Since he was gathering and punching the lead along, I just threw in on the drag. He had these cattle strung out quite a-ways, and it would take him an hour or so to work all the way back to where I rode. Sometimes his dog came along and sometimes the dog stayed up by the lead working all by himself. The first time Boyd rode back by me he didn't even look at me. I could tell I was doing a good job of living down to his expectations. This went on all day. I got pretty tired of his silent treatment and was very hungry.

His style and outfit sure weren't much to brag about. His kinky rope was tied on his worn-out saddle with a piece of orange twine, his old black felt hat didn't have a shape, and his horse had his head down in the grass half the time. I heard him yell at the cows and curse his dog in the distance. He had a voice like old gravel. I noticed he looked down at the top of his saddle most of the day and seemed always in deep thought. He only peered around once in awhile to look for cows or check on the progress of his dog. He and his dog Ring got along like a crabby old married couple. Instead of a normal dog/master relationship, the dog went where he damn well wanted whenever he pleased. The dog was as good as two cowboys, though, because he usually worked in just the right place at the perfect time. When that dog was happy with the progress of the cattle drive and felt like things were in order, he'd go lay down for a while. This habit, along with various differences on the correct way and speed to move cattle, fostered a lot of arguments between these two. When the dog decided to go a different way than Boyd, he'd bark in the face of the cattle to turn the lead. If Boyd wouldn't let him, Ring would go lay down and pout.

When Boyd swore and screamed too much, his dog just started for home. Eventually Boyd would remember how much easier it went with his dog and he'd sweet-talk him back. They would fight and make up like this a couple times a day. They made a very effective team, though. I've still never seen one man move so many cattle so smoothly. He always rode with a very loose rein, and his horse sure knew what to do.

Boyd's strategy on pretty much everything including horse training seemed to be to let time teach the way. If a young horse he was riding let a cow get by, Boyd didn't make a big deal about it. He just rode back around the cow no matter how long it took or how many times it took.

Before long the horse had it figured out that a couple quick steps now saved a whole lot of steps later. He just sat on that horse behind cattle for so long that the horse didn't have any choice but to learn, and Boyd just stayed out of his way. He gave his horses time. He gave cattle time, and he sure gave people time. I suppose eighteen years in prison benefits you with a fair perspective of that, and one thing I learned from him was that you had however much time it took to do the job. He did not know or care if it was Monday, Christmas, or nineteen ninety-nine, and he appeared absolutely indifferent whether he happened to be moving cattle at seven in the morning or eleven at night. "What's time to a cow?" he would say.

To move the cattle most of us cowboys shout something like: "***HUP, LET'S GO, HO CATTLE* or *HIKE ALONG, SISTERS*.**" Boyd would yell "***SAAAAAA***." He wasn't an Indian, like I thought when I first saw him, but he had been raised by a family of Blackfeet. He had copied many of their habits. Saaaaa was a pretty universal term in many tribes for "leave," "get out of here," and "GO NOW." We used to hear some of the old men who had trailed cattle with the Indians yell the same thing.

I had resolved not to talk to him until he spoke to me, but it started to get dark. We were still pushing the big herd and, on one of his hourly passes by me, I said, "Just where are we going with these cattle?"

" You're in the drag, kid; you don't need to know. I'll tell you when we get there."

We didn't get all those cattle anywhere in particular except north; and not long after he had finally spoken to me, we started back. He then cooked us a dinner and visited as if we were old friends. I learned that Boyd either felt like visiting or not, and you were way better off to let him initiate any type of conversation.

He usually didn't talk much during the day unless he had a particular instruction or plan pertinent to cattle. We would, however, sit up late most nights, and he would captivate me with stories of the old days and the old ways. I probably wouldn't be as impressed with him today as back then when I was so young. But, I really grew to care for that old man. I was forever trying to win his approval and tried really hard not to screw up around him in any fashion. When he got mad at one of us, he screamed out reams of abuse, that is, if he liked you. Otherwise, he just did a big sullen silent treatment. I really learned a lot from Boyd and he really kept you sharp.

"Think. Use your head. Look around. Dammit, kid, think!"

He said those words a million times, and we all dreaded his wrath. He was one of those old soldiers who enjoyed the battle more than the victory. If the present bovine-related activity happened to be going smoothly (for someone besides him), he warned and scolded that it was just some temporary bit of dumb luck that wouldn't last. He wore an air of indifference and didn't care a bit if anyone liked or approved of him. We young bucks who worked with him seemed to take it as a challenge to stay on his good side, and somehow his aloof attitude made him very appealing. The rest of us cowboys would be handing out compliments and shaking hands. No one cared a hoot about us. Boyd would go to a corner to sit by himself and pretty quick he had a whole crowd gathered.

Boyd's right leg was a couple inches shorter than the left. He had gotten shot in the leg during one of his escape attempts over by Kellogg, Idaho. The big femur bone grew back together side by side instead of end to end. It didn't bother him much because he rode a horse almost all the time anyway and he just shortened his right stirrup. He traveled OK going the right way on a steep side-hill, but otherwise he limped pretty badly.

As it got closer to fall, we started spending more time down at the main ranch, working cattle to ship. I shared a bunkhouse with several other cowboys in various stages of maturity and depreciation. The hard work and cold winds took their toll. The harsh elements were almost as detrimental as the self-inflicted, and mostly liquid, late night abuse of the local Mint Bar. The ranch was only three miles from the little town of Martinsdale and consequently the bar. We drank our beer and played pool under the stale gaze of eleven sad-eyed old mule deer heads, dark and dull from age. Each mount sported a great set of antlers and the name of the rancher who had vanquished him. We would go to the neon lights every night like a bunch of thirsty moths to drink barley-based beverages and rehash the events of the day. Then the next day, we would spend a fair part of our time rehashing the events in the bar the night before. It was our universe. Our boss could have just as well sent our pay to the bar directly and saved some paperwork. After awhile, we had a look in our eye about as bright as the cows we chased.

The bar owner was a tough old dry named Eldora. The story goes that she had arrived in the country with a cattle buyer one summer about twenty years ago. After they got in a lover's fight in which she allegedly knocked him out from under his toupee, he and his Cadillac left town without her. She had proven to be very resourceful, though, and came to own the best business in town. She fought off age with a sixties doo and a Clairol raven tint that matched the color of her heart. As far as we knew, she had been through three pickups, four poodles, and two husbands. Her pickups having slightly more trade-in value than her husbands, when she was through driving 'em. She was also one of the only five or so unattached women in about a three hundred square mile radius, so she had quite a working advantage. Sir Walter Raleigh wouldn't have treated those gals any better than we did up there.

She still had a fair figure and I think was probably quite a catch when she was young, but somewhere got sidetracked on the fashion train and looked like all her clothes were made from seat covers. The daylight was not her friend and highlighted her character pretty severely. She must have been aware of this fact because she mostly avoided direct sunlight and kept her activities nocturnal. She did not have a kind eye. It had an awful lot of white around it and she carried her nose a bit too high. Her manner always reminded me of a spooky old Arab mare that you wouldn't turn your back on, and you got the feeling she might just up and run over the ridge at a moment's notice. I could tell from the way she sneered that she had gotten pretty soured on men over the years. The word around town was: you would be safer trying to welsh on a Mafia-backed gambling debt than to be late paying your bar tab.

Her and Boyd were sort of an item and traveled together some when he came in out of the hills. Boyd tried to act cool as always, but you could tell he had the hots for Eldora. Whenever he was around her, he talked too much and the rowels on his spurs would start to turn on their own accord. If she wore one of her tight polyester cowgirl outfits, it looked like Boyd had little buzz-saws on his heels. It was not an exclusive relationship, however, and led to some pretty exciting times in town. We had drive-by shootings and road rage before anyone even knew what it was called.

The closest law was at least thirty-five miles of bad road away. So, if you expected justice, it took some patience. Unless someone needed serious hospitalization, we usually just had our own solutions.

"Somebody get him outta' here and lock the door for awhile," or, " Let's just tape it up and buy him a drink," would solve most problems.

When I hired on, I had brought my two horses and an old mule I owned. The ranch pastured them so I felt obligated to use them as much as possible. I rode my own horses until they were awfully pulled down. We planned to go on a big gather the next day. My young horses were so thin I was already ashamed of myself, so I decided to try my gangly old sorrel mule, "Harry."

I had gotten Harry, and his long head, on trade with a horse deal I made three years before. He was very skinny and even after I wormed and fed him, he would never lose his rough winter hair -- hence the name. I had meant to sell him as soon as he gained some weight and looked presentable; but no matter how much or what I fed him, he always looked like a starved greyhound after a tough bout of chemotherapy. He was very good-natured; however, so I hoped he could just get me to the vicinity of the cattle and I could send my good dog around to run 'em off the ridges.

I had ridden him around a little in the corral to make sure I could turn and stop him. I wanted to prove to the other cowboys I could use my mule. My ego got involved, and I got plenty of teasing from the other cowboys when I loaded him in the trailer to leave.

We were to gather in the big pasture called Moss Agate which runs along the highway between Ringling and White Sulphur Springs on the east side of the road. You can still see a big set of pole corrals there that they use to this day. The Moss Agate pasture ran north and south with some steep piney ridges coming in from the east and is named after a particular rock in that part of the country.

It belonged to my boss's brother, Ben, a fellow about my age. I had always wanted to meet him because from the stories around the country he sounded like he would be a fun friend to have. We set out to gather the ridges pushing the cattle down and work toward the north where Ben and his crew would be coming from.

It was shipping time and we wanted to work the cattle as quietly as possible so we wouldn't run off any extra weight. I had a heck of a time pulling and spurring Harry away from the rest of the crew. Since he had been a pack mule all his life and not used to being away from other horses, he sure didn't like it. I had managed to goad him to the top of a ridge and ordered my dog around to move some cows. It was one of those rare, nice, frosty mornings with no wind where the cattle really feel like moving. I would holler and send my dog their way, and they would go running and bucking down the mountain.

Harry and I spotted Ben coming down country with his cattle at the same time. My mule had realized he had made a terrible mistake letting himself get separated and had been constantly braying since we left. At sight of Ben's horse, he capitalized on his chance to be re-united with a horse and bolted straight toward him rocketing down the mountain. It was like trying to stop a Burlington Northern locomotive with a set of reins. We went crashing through trees and over small cliffs with me pulling back for all I was worth. It was, at best, terrifying and I would have jumped off, but I figured I could ride just as fast as this stupid S.O.B. could run, and the flying dismount option appeared like it would be just as painful as the thrashing I took being smeared through the tree branches. I gave up on one rein and tried to pull his head around to the side with both hands to slow or at least circle him. Being highly motivated, I managed to pull his nose clear up to my lap. Harry must have not liked the death-defying view any more than me, because I noticed he had the eye that was toward me clamped tightly shut.

We broke out of the trees and thundered out on to the flat country below us still going nine – O, heading straight at Ben and his herd of cattle. He was coming up quickly on our left and unfortunately I had Harry's head pulled around to the right.

Ben had stopped his horse and he grabbed his saddle. His jaw was hanging open and evidently his horse must have been unaccustomed to mules, because it appeared a bit skittish and had his eyes all bugged out. Also, he reared and whirled around a couple times trying desperately to leave the scene. I could tell from the way things were going that I wouldn't have much of an opportunity to visit.

"You never have a second chance to make a good first impression," I always say, so I tried to time it so that I could achieve my brief but friendly greeting while I was within voice range of Ben.

"*HELLO. I'M SKIP HALMES -- AND THIS IS MY MULE ---- H A I R R r e e e e e e e e e e ee e.*"

Well, I finally let his head go and we got er' shut down out on a fence corner on the north end. When I got back to the herd, I saw a real mess. I had spooked a bunch of the cattle with my run-away and the mother cows panicked and went back to the last place they had seen their calves, which was basically where we had started. They said later that Ben was able to track my progress through the thick timber on Harry by watching the top of the trees violently shaking. That may have been true, but this story took on a life of its own afterwards. Exaggerations spawned over strong drinks and mean spirits led to the telling of lies like brain damage and permanent finger-grips imbedded in my saddle horn.

I will concede there may have been some deep scratches on my cantle from my fingernails and I was a tad jumpy afterward, but the part about a petrified pine squirrel clinging to my stirrup leather and trying to help me pull on the reins was an outright falsehood. Those lies were only told to get my goat and besmirch my good name.

The other cowboys laughed about my wild ride down the mountain, but my boss and Boyd sure didn't. He was way too mad to scream at me, and I stayed pretty much invisible to him for a long time. I had broken a cardinal rule of stockmen by scattering that herd, and I didn't know if there would ever be a statute of limitations. Thinking back, it would have probably been easier to just move away and change my name. I wanted so bad to be known as good help and a top hand that I vowed to somehow live down or out-work my stained reputation. I wasn't about to be remembered as a dink and prayed every morning to be handy and go the extra mile. I avoided the Mint for a while because I couldn't stand the teasing. My favorite friend to B.S. with had been Boyd anyway, and now he wasn't even speaking to me.

I really minded my Ps and Qs at work and finally the other cowboys let up on me. I started going back to the Mint some evenings but didn't stay as late and was a lot sharper during the day. Eldora nicknamed me Mario Andretti after she heard the recantation of the story. Her brain was so fried she thought he was a famous jockey instead of a racecar driver. It all helped me out in the end because I got to thinking why the hell am I so worried about impressing these folks anyway?

An old Angus bull up the river from the ranch buildings would not come out of the brush. That part of the Musselshell River has lots of thick willows, and we had tried to get him several times with no luck. He wouldn't get out to where we could rope him, and he'd just bail-up and fight the horses. The boss really wanted him in the corral and one of the cowboys even tried using bird-shot. That only succeeded in making the bull even more belligerent and pissed-off than before

One Sunday afternoon, down by the barn I noticed one of the heifers was riding an old cow that had calved late. I got to thinking that if I could get that old cow, that was in season, somewhere upwind of that bull he just might want to come out of the brush. I caught a good horse and drove that cow up there after I locked her calf in the corral. It worked better than I could have hoped for, and the bull came right after her. I just backed off and the cow went at a run back to her calf with the bull right behind. The whole deal didn't take twenty minutes. I didn't say anything, and the next morning at the cookhouse Errol asked, "Who got the bull in?"

I told him how I did it and tried to be cool and nonchalant. Well, it was a pretty good day for me, and I knew I was probably back in Boyd's good graces. The funny thing was it didn't seem to matter that much anymore.

I had learned a lot about being a cowboy from Boyd. Like how to walk right behind a snorty filly without getting kicked. (You get in close and rest your hand on the top of her rump while you walk around.) Like how much wiser it is to lead cattle than it is to push them, and like how with training up a colt the way that seems slow is the fastest in the end. I also learned that lots of these methods applied to people as well.

Unless her name is Eldora.—She booted me clear across the dance floor.

Mostly I learned about life, and that it wasn't in me to remain content laboring on someone else's land and chasing another man's cattle. I wanted a ranch and family of my own. With that, I began working in earnest toward that end, and I have been greatly blessed.

1st Corinthians 13:11

Getting Started

I met Holly at a dance. In those days I drank a lot of beer and I noticed in my frequent trips to the rest room that I became proportionately better looking with the amount of alcohol I consumed. I was about at the point where I determined I was irresistible so I asked the prettiest girl in the place to dance with me. I noticed that she was about eye level as I approached her across the crowded noisy room. Only she was sitting down.

"Wanna' dance?" I asked.

"I'm pretty tall." She said.

"Oh, I don't mind." I said. "I've danced with lots of girls taller than me."

"I'll bet you have."

Well, I must have done a pretty good job on the dance floor because afterward I gave her one of the new business cards I had been issued and said, "Give me a call sometime, Polly."

I had to be pretty proactive to get on her good side after that. I can understand how in a moment of poor judgment she might have agreed to a date, but I still can't believe she married me.

We have been married for twenty years. This is quite a testament to Holly's resolve. I know a lot of couples who didn't last as long as the toasters they got for wedding gifts.

While Holly and I were dating, I was working at the worst job I've ever had. My employer was a cousin who owned a small brokerage with three other employees. My duties there were to make coffee, post the latest news stories off an old teletype machine, answer the phone, and do the books. I had to be there early because the markets opened two time zones east of us, and the farmers and ranchers who phoned in for quotes expected someone there. The deal with my cousin was for me to work for free for four months. I was to learn the business and then I would start to draw a small hourly wage. I was also studying so I could pass the difficult test that was necessary to become a broker. The fifth month of my employment the firm I worked for merged with another. The other firm brought in their own office workers. I lost my subsistence paycheck after only one month, and my compensation went to commission only.

This was a starve-to-death deal. Getting started as a broker takes some time and the only reason I didn't quit was I couldn't get another job. Not many people want to trust their money to an inexperienced young start-up wearing a black cowboy hat. First, I sold my four horses one by one. I frittered this money away on food and rent. No one would buy the skinny old mule I had left. Without horses I didn't need a stock trailer; so when I came to the end of my funds, I sold it, too. Who needs a truck if you don't own a trailer? I decided I could get by with a car, and I started looking for dependable cheap transportation.

In my search for a vehicle I met an old guy who was the executor of his aunt's estate, and he had to sell her old car to settle her affairs.

We came to an agreement on price, and part of the deal was he would open up a brokerage account with me. He was my first customer. His deceased aunt had evidently been quite myopic. It also could have been that she was attempting to widen out the doorway of her narrow garage by using the car for a battering ram. Besides the rounded-off corners, another feature of the old sedan was that it leaked badly around the windows and doors.

"It's a good thing that they don't build boats," I told my client after I owned it through the rainy spring season.

Unless we were well into a drought or suffering through a hard freeze, the odor of the mildewed carpet and damp seats reeked worse than rank socks. Whenever I could I asked people if they wouldn't mind smoking inside of the car, because it improved the smell. My seventy-one Buick Skylark sported an oxidized olive green paint job that clashed badly with the rust and white caulk that I kept applying around the windows. It was built like a tank and also rode like one. My cowboy buddies really teased me about my ride and labeled it.

"Amour De Bomba –The Love Machine"

Real funny. Ha- ha. When it comes to my plights – everyone was a comedian.

I was at this low point in my life when I met Holly's folks. She was way out of my league. She was a pretty young girl with a good job who was also very nice, while I was "inbetween opportunities" and looked like an accident involving Roy Rogers and one of the Hobbits. I'm a stocky little dark-haired guy while she is a lanky blonde. I told my friends, "We'd be a good Charolais-Angus cross." She was the youngest and favorite of six children. Her parents thought she could do better. Much better.

She took me out to meet her family on an Easter Sunday. I would say that the best description of her mother's reaction to me was, "openly hostile." Her dad regarded me with indifference. I think he had warmed to me some by my third visit because he tried to entice his dogs to play with me as soon as I got out of my car.

"Get him, Rex. Go get him!" he shouted.

After a year of dating, I was determined to propose. I intended to do this on her birthday in December. I wanted to do things right and give her a big diamond. I also figured she might have to be liquored up a bit to agree to a lifetime with me. I had a friend who owned a pawn shop and he would sell me a five thousand dollar diamond for thirty-five hundred. I budgeted for a nice dinner and I didn't want to take my own stinky car. I called a fellow from a mortuary that I knew so I could hire a limousine.

I started saving all I could and by the end of November I only had two thousand dollars. The only banker I knew was the nice lady I called when I couldn't make my monthly college loan payment. Rosalie Hall. I made an appointment to try for a loan.

"I need seventeen hundred dollars by Saturday," I told Rosalie and explained what the money was for.

"That's fine," She said. I felt like she was excited for me and wanted to be a part of this important occasion. "What do you have for collateral?"

"I have a car that's paid for," I said and handed her the title.

She took the title and was gone for fifteen minutes. She had a grim look of concern and was rubbing her right temple when she came back.

"They will only loan two hundred and fifty-seven dollars on your car, but we can still do this," she said with apprehension. "Do you have anything else free and clear that you could borrow on?"

My mind raced. I crossed my fingers under the table and said, "I have a really good mule."

She frowned and looked back at the loan application.

"I don't think we've ever loaned money on a mule before."

I stared outside and tried to think of anything else I could borrow on or any other way I could get the money. I had already lined my friend up to drive the limousine.

"He's a really good mule," I said and waited and waited some more.

She frowned again.

"Well, they're going to laugh when they see this one upstairs," she said, "but I think they'll do it on recommendation. You've always been honest with me." She paused while I held my breath and smiled, "Congratulations."

The evening was great and we had a lot of fun. The only blunder was when I was showing off my rented limousine at the Cowboy's Bar. The one-man band in the corner had deduced from all the excitement and my friends buying me drinks that we had gotten engaged. The singer then crooned out the Ann Murray tune, "Can I Have This Dance for the Rest of My Life?" Unfortunately this happened while I was outside with my friends and the uniformed limo driver. Holly was alone so an old drunken cowboy asked her to dance and she did. Then all the old cowboy's friends made the mistaken assumption that he was the one engaged to the beautiful young girl. We came in while they were all cheering at the end of the dance.

"By golly, Hector. You really done good. She's a looker."

Holly's mom, Joan, became quite emotional when we announced our plans of marriage. Her dad just resigned himself to the impending matrimony as one might deal with arthritis or an extended recession of the economy. It has been very easy to exceed their expectations of me.

I know Joan wore out a couple sets of rosary beads in fervent prayer that something would go awry in our romance. She is a discerning lady who loves her children fiercely and always did her best to set them up for success. Holly's dad is a good friend of mine now and even then he never tried to sway her decision one way or another. His only words of advice were, "If you're going to marry this guy, you're going to need a real good job."

My groomsmen were all going to rent their own tuxedos. The general process for this is to go to the men's store, get measured, and then they do a final fitting the day before the wedding. One of the friends standing up for me was Boyd. He sure wasn't going to come all the way over here to get measured so I had his boss's wife measure him once when he came down from his cow camp. The men's store sent instructions that we mailed up there and then they sent the measurements back.

The store couldn't reach me so they called Holly's number. She lived with her folks. Her mom answered the phone.

"Hello, this is Beatrice from the tuxedo rental service."

"Yes," Holly's mom said.

"Well, there seems to be a mistake in the measurement for one of the groomsmen in the Halmes' wedding party," Beatrice said.

"What kind of mistake?" Holly's mom asked.

"Well, one of the gentlemen sent in measurements that indicate his right leg is two inches shorter than his left leg," Beatrice explained.

"That sounds like a mistake alright," Holly's mom said. "I'll find out and have Skip call you."

We were well into the final stages of planning, and I was out at Holly's folks place that evening. Joan gave me a weather eye and said, "The men's store called about a mistake sent in on a tuxedo measurement." She then relayed the call.

I briefly thought about telling her that Boyd had been shot in the right leg escaping from prison the second time. I concluded that this explanation of my friend's physical impairment might re-enforce her already low opinion of my character.

"How about that?" I winced more than I meant to and jumped in my chair a little. I knew this wasn't a done deal yet and that a lot had to go just right before the sale was all the way closed. Then Holly would be legally obligated, and the "in sickness, health and death do us part," clause could work in my favor.

"It's always something," I said. "I'll give 'em a call tomorrow."

Boyd got to town for the rehearsal dinner two weeks later. He only came to town about every four months. His standard practice for this was to draw all of his back pay and then get the check cashed at the first bar he came to. He would always put enough money to get home in his left front shirt pocket. He put all of the other cash in his right. He then partied like a rock star until that pocket was empty. The process usually took about three days.

He had been deep into his heart pocket by the time he arrived late at our very traditional Catholic Church for the wedding rehearsal. He slouched into the cathedral and walked directly to the priest standing by Joan. The first thing he asked Father Dobbin was, "Where does a guy take a leak in here?" Boyd danced from leg to leg while he waited for the Father's gasping to stop.

Then he reminded them. "Hey, I have got to go pretty soon."

Our Father Dobbin was a somber Catholic of the grim old school. He had always believed Vatican Two was for sissies and that any frivolity was the devil's work. He and Holly's mom nodded to each other knowingly, and he appeared to now have bad gas pains along with a progressing nervous tick in his right eye.

We took Boyd to the fitting room at the men's store so he could try on his tux. Superman never made a bigger transformation than Boyd did when he came out of that small fitting booth. He went in all sloppy with his old flannel shirt untucked outside of his faded Levis. He came out looking like a Texas oil man. Boyd knew he looked good and he was determined to get his sixty dollars worth of use out of that suit. He wore it the rest of the weekend, shiny black shoes and all.

Keeping all the relatives in one spot without a fist fight long enough to get this done was quite a feat. I worried right to the end that I would forget something or mess up my lines. I will tell you it's hard to hold your breath that long.

My sister had hired a buggy for my bride and me for the trip to the reception at the V.F.W. hall. We were able to rent it for a very reasonable sum because my dad had been in the Army and Holly's brother provided a good band. My mom bought drinks for the house for awhile, and the wedding, dance, and party turned out great.

I had let Boyd take my car. He hadn't had a license for years and wound up in jail because he sideswiped a taxi leaving the church. He did a lot of damage to the other car but no one got hurt, and I couldn't even tell which one of the dents in my rig was from the taxi.

"That guy could have missed me if he would have tried at all," Boyd said.

When the policeman filing the accident report questioned Boyd he asked him. "Are you drunk?"

"As a Skunk." Boyd said.

Incredulous, the policeman inquired. "Don't you want to take the test or something?"

"Hell no. I already know I'm drunk. What would I want to take a test for?"

My friend, an former boss Errol, ended up posting bail..

We went elk hunting in the Bob Marshall Wilderness for our honeymoon and then went out to Seattle for a few days. Holly had won the trip that summer that included airfare and a nice hotel stay.

I had dropped the apartment I was renting because we had made a down payment on a used mobile home. We gypsied around for a couple weeks while we got it set up for occupancy. Holly and I stayed with various friends and relatives. In this time I discerned that you were welcom a little longer if you didn't do laundry or eat too much at the same place you were sleeping. So, most evenings we would go "visit someone" about dinnertime and take along our dirty clothes. Lots of people were good to us.

That trailer house was sold to us with the "special arctic package" feature that we understood provided for extra insulation and thermal windows. We figured out later it must mean that you had to dress like an Eskimo all winter. The thing also had an electric furnace that dimmed the lights when it kicked on. We made sure it didn't kick on too often. One January our electric bill was one half of my take-home pay.

Once Holly got through nurses' training we were in good shape financially because she immediately had a good job with benefits. We were able to save her whole paycheck every month and started looking for a place of our own.

Land was not as expensive in Montana in those years, and we found a perfect piece of property with a house and horse barn. Even though it had been abandoned for awhile, the basics were all there. It just needed someone to love it, and we still do.

Ecclesiastes 4:9-12

The Hodson Cattle

When we first got started in the cattle business, we were really scared when it came time to borrow the money. We didn't have any rich uncles or family to back us, so we had to borrow from Farm Credit Services. They were very conservative and cautious because they had had just come off some awfully hard years in the Ag Lending industry. We filled out reams of forms and documents. They were understandably skeptical and scrutinized our plan closely because, of course, we were unproven with an untested loan history and no financial reserves.

What we did to get started was to buy good-sized old bred cows by the head in the spring. We could usually get them for hamburger price. We would let the cows calve, summer them on good pasture, and then resell them by the pound as soon as the calves could be weaned. That way the calf was mostly profit. My main criteria when choosing my cattle was that they be dirt cheap. I would buy cattle that very few other people wanted and get along with them the best we could. It was a good system and a great way for a young couple to get started. There was very little market risk, and those old cows have seen it all and do a good job of taking care of themselves. I got a lot of teasing from the neighbors about my raggedy cow herd, but they always paid the bank back and then some.

The third year we tried this we bought some old cows from John Lane. He is a friend and neighbor to the south.

He stopped by on his way to a big pasture he leases above our place when I was out in the barn shoeing one of the horses I had tied up.

"Are you looking for any short-term cows this fall?" he asked.

"I don't know. I might get some. How many do you have?"

"About thirty – they're pretty high headed. I'll tell you that, but they always bring in a big calf. These would be the tail end of those Hodson cattle we got with the place that we never quite got loaded before. Dad said to get rid of 'em before they hurt somebody. I'll make you a heck of a deal," he said.

"I'll have to talk to the bank and Holly. It's gonna' be easier convincing the bank than it will her. She always thinks I'm gonna' break us on one of my cow deals. How much would they cost?" I asked.

My old mule "Harry" had walked up to the trough we were by, hoping for a hand-out. He had always looked so pitiful it was tough not to feed him whenever there was a chance so I got him some oats while we were talking.

"Oh, we'll price em' right. That's quite an animal. Where did you happen by him?" John asked.

"Way back. I guess about eleven years ago when I was still in college. I got him in a horse trade. I traded one good gelding for two horses and two mules. A one-for-four deal. The two horses were full brothers. Good looking sorrel geldings. One was just started and he turned out real good. I owned him for years.

His brother was a year younger and better looking, but the most dangerous horse for kicking I was ever around. I never could get anything done with him and ended up selling him as a bucking horse to a stock contractor in Ennis. I sold the one mule right away as a pack mule, and this one was really skinny but gentle and I kinda' started liking him."

John looked at me as if my explanation wasn't quite complete so I went on.

"I was always going to fatten him up and sell him, too, for packing, but I never could get much weight on him. I tried everything," I explained.

I think John was searching for some supportive comment as he looked back at Harry.

"That's alright, by God. I hate a quitter," he said.

We bought the cows. They were some of the last cattle that came with the ranch his family had purchased up in this country and showed a little horn and a lot of attitude. The cattle had been born and bred in the high, rough country fighting off bears and coyotes; they were wild as elk, and you wouldn't dare get in a pen with 'em unless your affairs were in order.

We had a bad episode of scours go through our caves the previous year so I was committed to inoculate every calf as soon as they were born. This turned out to be a very bad idea especially with this set of cows. Most of these cattle only watered at night and would never leave their calves in the day. You can well imagine the advantage of giving the shot without the mother cow in attendance. After a couple days the calves had the mobility of young antelope so catching them was really tough.

One black white-faced cow was really honky. She would chase your horse or the truck if you got too close, and she never seemed to leave her calf to eat hay or get a drink. I was going into town to get the mail about noon one day, and I spotted her calf lying down without the Hell-Bitch anywhere in sight. I stopped and took my syringe out there and smugly administered the dose while he bawled his little head off. I was feeling pretty good about the attributes of patience and persistence when I heard a faint thundering sound. Here she came and there I went, as fast as you can run in cowboy boots, toward my truck parked out on the county road.

Any other cow would have went over to check on her calf first, but this old hide had retribution as a priority and headed straight toward me, cutting the corner. Evidently in Satan's school for cows, one class they teach besides fence crawling and cowboy maiming, is geometry. This cow certainly was capitalizing on her knowledge of the closest distance between two points. It was like a Montana version of running with the bulls. I just made it under the fence and was panting like a wind-broke horse out at the county road. John Lane happened to be on his way up to his pasture and stopped his truck to visit. He could see the cow blowing snot and just daring me to get back on her side of the fence. Of course, I couldn't talk having just done the wind sprint of my life.

John is unfazed and says, "She sure is a good mother, isn't she?"

I got along alright with these cattle until the last one calved and she was just as snorty. I had been trying to think of a different strategy. I thought what might work was to rope the calf off my horse, drag it over to the fence, and tie my rope to the top of a post while I was still on my horse. I was then going to ride way down the fence and leave my horse there while I came back up the fence on the safe side. That way I could pull the calf under the bottom wire and give him his shot.

Like I say, I'm a slow learner. The cow figured out what I was up to. The devious old witch first went way down the fence and hooked my horse until he broke the reins and headed home. When she was satisfied that she had me stranded on foot, she came back. I was still trying to get the calf pulled under the fence when she got there. At that point I surmised that the flimsy eighty-year-old four-wire fence just might not keep her away from me when that calf really got to raising hell. Where is Lassie when you need her? I have always been very spiritual at such times and started talking to the Lord.

"God, if you just let me have my rope back and don't let this cow kill me, I promise I'll swear off this givin' all the calves a shot business."

I had experienced the coincidence of deep prayer and deep sh_t before. so at least I was in familiar territory. About then Holly bounced up in the pickup and ran the cow off by bumping her hard with the heavy grill guard. My horse running home without me had tipped her off.

I took this as a sign that God had been listening so I stayed true to my word with him and we have all been a lot happier.

We had some of these cows around for several years and we got along OK as long as we mostly left them alone. These cows always raised a big calf for us and I grew to respect them. The last one we had was so boney and old that I didn't think she would be worth hauling to town and I also figured she was bred again. My plan was to let her raise her calf until the next fall and then send her to the hereafter.

She was old enough that I didn't want to trail her home the ten miles from our summer pasture lease. I got her into an old hay corral out at the pasture and backed the stock trailer into the gate on one end.

I was on crutches that whole summer so I convinced Holly to try to load the cow. She promptly ran Holly out. We had to make the deal work pretty soon because the old hay corral was not going to hold her for long. "Holly, just try to ease her this way to the corner of the pen and the open door of the trailer. I'll get in there and when she tries to come back, I'll hit her in the nose with this shovel," I said.

"Don't you have a plan B? You're on crutches. This is stupid; you won't be able to get out of her way if you need to," she replied.

"This is plan A,B,C and D, and I'm not going to get out of her way. Don't worry, Honey. It's an old horse whisperer technique. Make the right thing easy and the wrong thing difficult - or painful. Besides I don't know what else to do?" I explained.

Holly did a great job of getting her up to the trailer and when that cow refused to load, she came right at me. I stood my ground and Babe Ruthed her in the snout with all the energy that a man with limited options can muster. It really made her old eyes water and she hopped right up in the trailer. She calved late the next year and we kept them in a pasture close to the house down on the creek. Her rat-tailed calf was just as wild as her, and they didn't seem to appreciate our stewardship at all.

My sons were about eleven and nine years old then, and a friend of theirs from school was staying with them over the weekend. I was fencing along the county road about a half a mile from the house on a cold windy day, and they hiked up there to see me. They visited awhile and then started for home, jostling with each other and just having fun. The old cow and her calf were quite a way off but when the boys cut through the pasture; she came right for them.

Some cows will bluff charge and only come so close and then just paw the dirt, bellow, and shake their head. This cow wasn't kidding and she meant to run those boys down. I was too far away to help and could only watch with horror as she came on.

The boys heard me hollering and for an awful moment looked toward me instead of the cow. They quickly figured out what I was yelling about and then went three different directions when they saw her coming. She zoned in on Jake and put her head down to hook him.

Luckily he was one of the fastest of the three boys, and he just made it to the fence and dived under. It tore his shirt and scratched him up a little when he slid under the barbed wire, but other than that he was fine. I was upset to say the least. When I got there and made sure everyone was okay, I coached Jake on some cow-evading techniques.

"Jake, when those cows are trying to run you down, you've got to make a few sharp turns. They get too good a run at ya' when you just go straight."

He was still pretty upset and informed me, "Once again, some information I could have used ***yesterday!***"

It was way too close and that cow was too dangerous to have around. I gathered up the boys and they were all excited and laughing when they recounted the story of their hilarious near-death experience. I wasn't laughing. I had been going to shoot that cow anyway, and now I was in the perfect mood for it. We got the gun, did the deed, and then drug her into a coulee with the pickup. I said a few words over her but not the kind I can repeat.

We took my son's friend home right after this and he told the whole story to his folks with special emphasis on how the cow died. They couldn't have known we were going to kill that cow anyway. From then on, the word around town was 'we don't take **any** crap off our cows out on the Lepley Creek Ranch.'

Proverbs 24:10

Driving Mrs. Daisy -- into Insanity

I have been driving my wife around for about twenty-two years, and it has taken quite a toll on both of us. We have had some very heated debates regarding the differences in our driving methods.

My wife wasn't always this antagonistic. When we were dating, she used to sit by me in my old car and was completely quiet. She wore a serene smile and appeared to be the picture of contentment. She might give my knee a gentle squeeze if she thought I was driving too fast on an icy road or when I was approaching a sharp curve. I used to rather enjoy the physical contact, and I often drove a little recklessly just for the effect.

Oh, for the bliss of yesteryear. Now she has plenty to say. She also waves her arms around in angry broad gestures as if she were conducting an orchestra. It has gotten to the point that sometimes I worry about losing an eye. Every so often while I'm driving merrily along, right out of the blue she will emit a horrible gasp. I naturally assume there's some prevailing danger that I'm unaware of and death is imminent. I slam on the brakes and look wildly around for the impending disaster. I rarely see anything of note.

"He might not have stopped for that sign you know," she says.

Part of the problem is that we have vastly different driving styles. She peers straight down the road and maintains a constant speed. There could be a forest fire on one side of the road and a tornado on the other and she would never know. When we drive into one of those heavy storms where it seems like your windshield is splitting a vortex of snow, she gets so nauseous and wall-eyed that she has to let me take over and lay back in the passenger seat with her eyes closed. It's just too much focus for her.

I don't suffer from that issue of focus. I like to see what's going on out in the country. I look on both sides of the road, watch above me for geese or airplanes, and I keep track of what's coming up behind me. I like to know if the neighbors have their bulls turned out, if they're done calving, the condition of the range, et cetera. When I get somewhere, I've got some news. If someone asks how the spring wheat is looking or if the deer have shed their horns yet, I can tell them. I always try to spot game; and if we are fortunate enough to be driving along a river, I watch for rising trout.

Something else that formed my driving style is that I grew up driving old ranch rigs. If you put a new dent or ding in them, there was a good chance no one would notice; and if you banged em' up a little bit, they probably had it coming. We use our vehicles hard and everything we own is a four-wheel drive.

There is a saying in Montana that - *the older our truck gets, the more places we are willing to take it* - and we own trucks that we will take anywhere. This attitude of not worrying too much over the treatment of my vehicle carries further than the ranch. When I'm in town, and I need to change lanes, I just put on the blinker, count to three, and pull over. If I want to stop at a store, I just slop into a parking area, pull ahead until something stops me, and call 'er good.

For Holly, aligning her car at the shopping mall is a precision maneuver, much like painting trim or brain surgery. Her rig is consistently clean and she keeps it well-maintained and orderly. This contrasts with my trashy pickups that may or may not get you where you're going. On our last trip to town she asked, "When is the last time you changed the oil in this?"

"I don't know. I think the guys at the dealership might have changed it when they extracted that antelope out of the fan belt last fall," I replied.

"Well, also there's a big breeze whistling in around the door and the wheels are shaking. Do you know what causes that awful whirring sound coming from the transmission?

"Not really," I said.

"This truck is only four years old. It should be in better shape," she said.

I gave my explanation.

"The door almost got tore off when that hunter let go of it in a high wind last fall, and we have to chain it up all the way around to get some of those elk out. I think that's pretty tough on the steering and alignment. I don't know how careful the boys are with it when they take it fencing or the guides are when they are using it, and we do pull some pretty big loads in the stock trailer once in awhile. It works pretty hard if you think about it."

I paused a while to think up some more past abuses.

"Rancher's truck years are longer than regular years. Sorta' like doggie years. So this truck is really closer to -- I'll say, twenty-eight years old."

She looked wistfully out at the passing countryside and said, "The same probably applies to rancher's wives. Why are we going so fast?"

"We are only going fifty-five. It just sounds like we're going fast."

She is a nurse and has a whole boatload of driving paranoia - like swerving into a river or other vehicles failing to stop at an intersection. She also fears brake failures, blowouts, meteor strikes, you name it. In Holly's judgment, anyone who passes her on the road is a lunatic, and whoever is in front of her impeding her progress is a "Grampa' Gumby." She loves to say the words **black ice** or **loose gravel,** and I have noticed that her eighty miles an hour is much more of a prudent speed than my own. It will not be a surprise to her if we ever die in a fiery crash. She's been predicting it for years.

When I get to heaven, even if I'm ninety-nine the first words I hear will be, "I knew this would happen. It was just a matter of time with all your gawking around and not paying attention that you got us killed."

The kids and I call her Little Miss Sunshine. She can prophesize a deeply perilous outcome for nearly any routine activity. Last week she told us, "One time I had a patient who slipped while she was holding some toe-nail clippers in her car, and she nearly died from the puncture wound."

I have been driving on gravel roads since I was eight. The worse the road is the better I drive. I do great on a badly drifted trail or some of the terrible washboard roads we drive every day. I have had a lot of practice and the skills for driving on gravel or logging trails are different than those for the interstate.

"Slow down! These roads are terrible," Holly said.

We were bouncing home on our rough pot-holed road and Holly thought I was traveling too fast for safety. "Why don't you just drive?" I said. "You drive all the time anyway, whether you're behind the wheel or not so you just as well be driving. That way we won't fight."

"Just slow down . Please." She pleaded. "I wonder why the county road grader never works on our road anymore. It's one solid washboard."

"Well he's got hundreds of miles of roads to keep track of, but really I don't remember the last time he was here.

Sometimes its worse when he's done anyway."

"Do you know Katie doesn't even believe in the road grader. You could just as well convince her that the Tooth Fairy or Big Foot is real," Holly said.

"Well she is only twelve. Maybe she'll see one before she gets out of high school."

I think interstates are just too easy for me. My mind tends to wander and I start multitasking. I listen to lots of books on tape, call my kids with chores, I try to close a cattle sale, or work on dialog for this book. If I'm really thinking hard or tired, I have to slow down. If I'm excited or late I drive pretty fast. I consistently look out my mirror to see what is approaching from the rear. If I see several cars gaining on me, I feel like I might be holding up traffic so I speed up. If there are a lot of them, I feel quite pushed and try to outrun them all. I have to admit this has been a problem in the past when we go out of state and hit a major freeway. One time on a family trip we hit Denver at rush hour. I believe if it weren't for the shoulder harness, Holly's wild gestures might have fluttered her right out of the car.

The route we take to achieve a destination is of major importance to Holly. She is efficient by nature and has strong feelings on this. I don't really care how people get where they're going, and I feel like *Hey- they're driving- they can get there the way they want to.* If someone wants to get to Texas from Montana by way of Florida, it doesn't bother me at all. Street numbers are also a tough concept for my mental G.P.S. I grew up out in big country. I could usually see the spot I wanted to end up at and could just travel that direction. If I wanted to go to Square Butte or Elk Ridge, I could just turn in the hubs or saddle up and head there.

If someone says, "I live on Twenty-Fifth Avenue North and Seventh - Street." I have a hard time visualizing that as a location. I have to ask, "What store is that by?"

They tell me, I get to the general location, and then work in smaller concentric routes until I home in on it. I am intimidated by big cities and it infuriates me when I can see a store I want to get to but the streets won't let me. Like most men, I always think I know where I'm going, and I am slow to accept the fact I'm lost or on the wrong track.

We recently got in a big fight trying to get to a friend's house in a new subdivision. I was having trouble finding it. We were arguing about the directions I had scribbled down. We were going to be late.

"Turn right here," she said.

I turned to the right and took out a mailbox.

"I didn't mean go right. I ment' turn in over there," she said.

"You said 'go right'. I went right. There is no pleasing you." I said. I felt I had already endured enough instruction for a lifetime.

"I'll get out and come around there, you slide over here behind the wheel, and then you can get there any damn way you want to. I am so sick of your driving directions that I can hardly stand it any more! The new rule in this pickup is: -- either shut-up or walk."

Note to self.

Be sure you're the one inside the vehicle when you decide to apply the new rule.

It could save you a long hike.

Philippians 2:14

Don't Tell Mom

We say that a lot around here. We've known for some time that forgiveness is easier to come by than permission when it comes to an activity of questionable judgment. On those occasions when our incautious behavior results in an injury to our person, some livestock, or a piece of equipment, I understand the benefit of keeping the incident quiet. Sometimes, though, my kids like to scare their mother with their tales of peril and enjoy the attention, even though they realize they will be subjected to a mandatory butt-chewing. I always get a double dose of berating because I should "know better."

You always hear how bad television is for kids. As you can tell from some of my stories, we thought up some stunts that were far worse for us than any T.V. show could have ever been. We turn our television off every summer and our kids think of some pretty creative ways to entertain themselves, too.

We were weaning some steer calves in the corral by the house about nine years ago. Jake was eight and Matt was six. They wanted to *go pet the calves.*

"Sure," I said. "I don't think you'll have much luck though. They're pretty wild."

Even though those calves were about six hundred pounds, I wasn't too worried because I was out on the porch where I could watch out for them while I was reading.

I was also pretty confident that they wouldn't be able to get anywhere near any of those rowdy calves.

They were just hazing them around into the corners of the big lot and having no luck in getting near them on any of the occasions I was watching so I mostly focused on the book I was reading. Once again, I had underestimated my children's resourcefulness when it came to getting themselves in trouble.

In this same lot were several calf feeders that had a type of prison bar arrangement about five feet out around their perimeter. The bars are designed to allow calves in but keep cows out. After Jake and Matt were unsuccessful cornering any calves, they schemed up a plan to perch on top of the feeder and for Matt to pounce on the first hungry steer that entered the iron barred enclosure. Matt weighed maybe fifty-five pounds. The steer objected vigorously to being "petted."

I heard the hollering and wailing and looked over to see Jake assisting his brother. Matt was crying and leaning on Jake like a wounded soldier while he limped back over to the porch.

"Man, you should have seen it," Jake said. "A big calf hit Matt and flipped him way up in the air - and he twirled around and landed right on his head."

Matt nodded vigorously in agreement through streaming tears. He seemed to take it quite personally that the steer didn't like or appreciate his attention. I checked him out for damage, and seeing nothing serious I held him in my lap until he felt a little better.

"Boy, I sure don't think we need to tell your mom about this deal when she gets home. Huh? I mean she'd just get upset and yell at us and there is no harm done. How about it, boys? Don't you think? How about a can a pop?"

They both nodded solemnly. Jake went inside and I continued to hold Matt and read my book. He felt better and eventually took a nap beside me out on the porch. About an hour later Holly got home from work, and I heard her car pull up to the driveway. Jake went running out the side door of the house to meet his mom before I could stop him.

"Guess what, Mom. A big steer hooked Matt thirty feet in the air. He did about ten flips; and when he finally came down, he smashed his head on a big rock!"

"Oh. Oh no! Where is he now?"

"He's out sleeping behind the house." Jake said.

"Sleeping! You mean he's unconscious?"

Holly has long legs and she vaulted the fence in front of the car. She took the five steps up to the porch in one jump. She glared at me murderously and lifted Matt off my chest where he had been laying.

I got a lecture and a loud tongue lashing that certainly did long-term damage to my ego; and if she could have found which steer did that to her little boy, that particular bovine would not have seen the sundown.

When I next saw Jake, I asked, "What happened to the - **don't tell Mom** – deal, Jake? I thought this was going to be our secret?"

"Oh ya'. . . Gee, I guess I forgot. . . Do ya' got any gum?"

"Forgot – forgot, man, I really got in trouble, Jake; and if I had any gum, I sure wouldn't give any to you. I would have put it in my ears a few minutes ago to protect my hearing and what's left of my self-esteem."

There's been a lot of that "don't tell Mom" business over the years.

"Katie, it sure wouldn't hurt anything if you kept quiet about when you were trying to head that cow off at a high lope by that cliff above the canyon." Or,

"Don't ever twist the rattles off a snake while he's still alive- ever again - even though you were standing on his head, Jake. And for the love of God, I beg of you, please don't tell your mother about this. Please, please, pretty please. She'll kill me."

My favorite story is not a *"don't tell Mom"* event, but is about the time Mom didn't tell.

We had both worked in town all day and were unloading groceries after a harried Monday and the forty-five minute drive out to our ranch. As soon as we got in the door, our seven-year-old Cub Scout, Jake, informed us we had to be to his troop's Christmas gift exchange in twenty minutes. As excited as he was, we decided it must constitute the social event of the season. According to him, attendance was of paramount importance and mandatory for advancement in the pack. This was our first notification of this gala event.

Of course, we didn't just happen to have any spare appropriate gifts for a boy of -*an approximate value of between five and fifteen dollars* - just laying around the ranch for this type of contingency.

"I just bought the boys new underwear. That'll have to do," Holly said.

"Underwear? As a gift?. . . I don't know, Holly, if that'll work," I said.

"They'll be fine. I'll wrap em' up really nice. It's all we've got anyway. We've got to get going," she replied.

By the time we got to the bustling scout party, Holly had second thoughts. She could recognize the package she wrapped among all the others. It was under the tree in the front of the room and she came up with a plan.

She leaned over and whispered, "Jake, just go pick the package that we brought. I think that's best."

Jake wasn't too happy with this deal but he obeyed his mother. He went to the tree and picked it up.

"Jake, honey, you can't pick your own gift," The den mother in charge of the gift exchange said. She had watched him put it down earlier. "Go ahead and pick something else."

"Ya Jake - geeeze' sweetie. Take something else," Holly, the dirtball traitor, said from the back of the room.

Jake was certainly confused but he liked the outcome. He shrugged his little shoulders and chose another gift. It was a red Swiss army knife. A million times better deal than underwear. The other kids were all opening neat stuff like games or action figures. His friend Thomas assumed that if Jake wanted it back, the gift must be really good so he chose our present.

My kids were all skinny little tykes at that age, and Jake weighed about sixty pounds soaking wet. Thomas was one of those cute little boys who grew out before he grew up and was at a pretty round stage of development. He tore open the package to find two tiny pair of plaid boxer shorts. They were obviously not a practical size. His expression betrayed extreme disappointment. Thomas's father saw his obvious anguish and scolded him.

"Thomas! Don't be unappreciative. Those are very nice underwear, and I am sure some little boy shopped very hard for them. Now be grateful for your gift."

Thomas picked up the underwear by the edges and looked sadly at them again and then held them by the edges and turned them around. Then he looked in the bottom of the box again. He was still speechless. It was as if he hoped that with time they might transform into something else, or the obvious injustice would be rectified. I only hope the traumatic experience didn't scar him for life so that he was afraid of opening Christmas presents from then on.

So we know about the situation that *Don't Tell Mom* applies and about the time *Mom didn't tell,* but most kids in a real crisis realize they need their mom A.S.A.P. When you are young, your mom can take care of pretty much anything. When someone is being picked on, you hear "I'll tell my Mom!" It is like their personal 911 alert or a call to Superman.

All of us kids knew, that in a real bad deal, a genuine root-hog or die crisis, we could depend on our mom..

Our neighbor John and his cousin Brian, when they were about eight years old, decided that they would halter break a bum calf that Brian had been feeding over the summer. The calf was in some corrals about three hundred yards from the house. They put him in the smallest pen and pulled him around for a little while. In a very short time, they felt they had him sufficiently compliant for a test. They decided to use the big three-acre lot to test their training.

Johnny and Brian knew they would be in hot water if they let the calf escape. They were still on probation from when they had gotten into trouble a month before.

That time they had fashioned a harness out of some baling twine and hitched up a saddle horse to Brian's wagon. For the maiden voyage, Brian was the passenger and John held the horse until he got started. Then he was going to get on, too. He never had that chance.

It had scared the poor animal so bad that he charged through the clothes line and then did four circuits of the pasture dragging the wreckage of their project. Brian only stayed in the wagon for part of the first round and then bounced out on his butt. When they named those little red wagons "Radio Flyers", little did they know.

"How come Brian was in the wagon and you weren't?" Brian's mom asked.

"It was his wagon," John explained.

Brian's mom ended up taking away the willow switch that John had been using as a buggy whip to snap the horse on the rump, and then she threatened him with it. They were in big time trouble and never did find all the parts to the wagon. With this memory quite fresh, Brian was voicing some concerns.

"What if the calf gets away?" Brian asked.

"We better tie the rope to your belt loop. That way you can't drop it," John said.

"Why my belt loop?"

"It's your calf," John said. "I'll open the gate."

As soon as the calf saw daylight, Brian had to sprint in dashing eight-foot strides to avoid being dragged. The calf was exercising his new freedom with great relish and wouldn't stop long enough for Brian to untie the rope.

They made about five laps in AAA time as John stood by.

"**Go get my mom**!" Brian screamed as he and the calf zoomed by on lap number six..

John had mixed feelings about this. When he finally walked over and went into the house he was fortunate enough to find his aunt napping so he sauntered back to the corral. Brian was pretty well broke to lead by the time John got back, and the calf was showing no signs of fatigue.

"**Where's my mom?**" Brian called when he saw John.

"**She's asleep**," John yelled back.

About then the calf jumped a salt trough and Brian didn't. His belt loop gave away and then they only had the problem of getting the halter off so their mischief wouldn't be discovered.

John 8:32

I Think My Days are Numbered

Events of late and some fresh contusions have led to my recent fears. My jumpy demeanor and paranoia are a legitimate response to these happenings; and should I die under mysterious circumstances, I want someone to question my wife.

Last month Holly, the kids, and I were up fixing fence in a canyon on our ranch and saw a big rattlesnake crawl down a gopher hole right by a gate post. I didn't want to be worrying and looking out for that snake every time we went through that gate so I was determined to kill him right then.

I had some gas for a chain saw we were using so I poured some down the hole hoping that would send him up for some air. I tried several treatments of this with no luck. Next, I took the post bar and shoved it way down the hole and rooted it around a bit. I was showing off some for the kids in the truck because they were watching with great interest. I remember using my Crocodile Hunter accent along with my poking and prodding.

"Thaaay reaaly hate it when you doo this. Put another shrimp on the barbee, mate."

All of a sudden that snake slithered up ready for battle and he was triple pissed off. He came right at me hissing and striking, and I backed up fast and tried fending him off with that big steel bar.

Holly had been waiting in the pickup with the window rolled down and the pistol ready to fire. She shot about the time the snake struck. Being highly motivated, I discovered that a forty-six year old man can achieve about seven feet of vertical lift. I also learned that by vigorously flapping your arms and kicking your legs you can delay your landing by three or four seconds. Because of the extreme danger and trauma of the situation, my memory might be a little jaded; but my recollection of these events are that every time I landed she shot. It was as perilous of situation as I have ever encountered. The snake was scary, too. I am pretty sure she kept shooting by my feet even after the snake was dead. I definitely remember what appeared to be a wild gleam in her eye.

The next event that aroused my suspicions happened two weeks ago. I had gone up to the hay loft of our barn to drop some hay down into the feeders. Our loft is set up with these trap doors that let you drop hay through the floor to the front of the horse stalls below. I noticed one of the doors was slightly ajar so I stomped on it to secure it in place. Instantly I'm a whole story lower and straddling the hay manger. Luckily the culprit hadn't gotten around to placing the sharpened pungi sticks with the poisoned tips on the bottom yet so the evil plan to bump me off was once again foiled.

My third level of distrust came about because my Aunt Janet happened to be inside the tanning booth at The Robin's Nest Beauty Salon last Tuesday. She overheard Robin and Holly running me, and Robin's husband, Jack, over the coals. Robin is the owner of the hometown hair salon and it is where most of the local gossip takes place. It is a cute building right on our main street and has an old-fashioned false front. The place is always clean and friendly; and since we don't have a local barber shop, it does a fair amount of business serving men, too. It is one of the more busy establishments of the dozen or so we have in our small town.

We had a heated debate earlier that same day, because I wanted her to do a couple errands in town since she was going anyway.

"I'm not going to the beauty shop with a dead elk in the back of the truck," she informed me.

"Well, you're always the one saying how we should try to save some gas and cut down on expenses around here."

She put her hands on her hips and said evenly, "You're not talking me into this today. I barely have time for the things I need to do and this is supposed to be a day of rest for me—my day off," Holly said.

"Well, the elk is already loaded, and I don't know how else you'll get to town, because the car isn't running very well. I wouldn't take a chance with it if I were you." She deftly adjusted the grip on the broom she was using and took a swipe at me.

I resorted to scripture. "The good book says wives should submit to their husbands," I exclaimed.

"How about if I submit a jab to your head? . . It's in the book of Tae-Boe."

"You know you're like that lady Martha in the Bible that Jesus scolded," I said.

"How so?" she asked.

"Remember she was in the kitchen getting lunch ready and her sister Mary was in the other room listening to Jesus teach instead of helping out. . . Martha complained, and then Jesus reminded her that Mary was doing the more important thing. Do you remember?" I said.

"Well - you know everybody always slams Martha, but at least she got her work done," she replied.

Since she didn't have much choice, and time was getting away, she left. Evidently she was still pretty mad by the time she got to her friend Robin's beauty shop. It was my good fortune that my Aunt Janet eavesdropped and she told me the whole story.

Robin could see right away that something was wrong when she got there and asked, "You're wearing way too much of that musk perfume. It's about to knock my hat off, and it looks like you got a little wild with your rouge today. What's going on?"

"My husband is really ticking me off," Holly rasped.

"Mine, too. You go first," Robin said.

"Well, to begin with it's not rouge; it's probably elk blood. Skip talked me into hauling to the game processors a bull elk that one of our hunters killed. I was going to drop it off before I came here. I ended up having to wrestle it around when I had to get the spare tire out from under it. The pickup had a flat on the way in here. That's why I'm late and it could also be why I might smell a little gamey."

Robin replied, "Last time you were here you were pulling that old stock trailer with some yearling steers in it. I remember because you ran over my pot of begonias out by the sign in the parking lot."

"Sorry about that. That old gooseneck really cuts the corners. I had Katie watching out the window for me when I pulled that thing out, but she didn't see those plants. That was the day I took those steers to the Wednesday sale at Western Livestock. He's big on me multi tasking and saving trips to town," Holly sighed.

"Why does Skip always call Katie Doc?" Robin asked.

"He wanted to name her Doc." Holly said. "Doc's Little Lena, actually. I had to really put my foot down or that's what she'd be stuck with."

"Doc's Little Lena?

"Ya, after a cuttin' horse mare he really likes. . . God help us," Holly said.

Holly was quiet while Robin washed her hair and had composed herself by the time Robin started cutting her bangs. Then she asked, "So, what has Jack been up to?"

"Well, you know all he ever does is work, and then he's too tired to be much company at night. Mostly he just falls asleep in front of the TV. His idea of a romantic evening is when we put salt out together; and for the last three years, he has taken his vacation time to go hunting," Robin said.

"We never take a vacation together either," Holly said.

"I thought you guys just went up to that bed and breakfast cottage on the Flathead for the weekend last month."

"We went to the Flathead alright or almost. You know we got that trip from Jill. Her friends own that cottage up there and she bought us the trip for helping her move out of her apartment two years ago."

"I remember that," Robin said.

"Well, Skip thought since we were going that way he would take a trailer along and we could pick up a load of poles for the corrals.

Then, the day we were going to leave, a water line broke and he worked on it till late at night so right there we're down to one day. I should have just stayed home," Holly explained. "We left early the next morning and there was no one at the stupid post yard when we got there. It took forever to get loaded, and we didn't get to our room until pretty late. The dinner part of our weekend package deal was over. It snowed that night so we thought we should get an early start home. It took forever. The roads were so bad that we ended up putting chains on just to get back over Roger's Pass. That was our *special weekend*... waa - hoo... Would have hated to miss that one."

"That's too bad. . I remember that storm. What did he get you for your birthday last week?"

"Hearing protector head phones with a radio built-in so I can listen to music while I am feeding in the tractor," Holly said softly.

"Where did he find those?" Robin asked.

"Big R Rancher's Supply. He does all his Christmas shopping there, too. He loves that place, and we have a charge account there. He says, *'They've got everything.'* Horse gear, feed, tools, guns and fishing tackle. He rides the shopping carts down the parking lot to the door, and I think he likes talking to all those cute country girls who work in there. Heck, if they had tap beer and a happy hour, he would never leave."

"You know I've been after Jack for us to spend some quality time together, too, so last spring he agreed to go with me to that weekly book club that the Reverend Johansen started," Robin said..

"I saw that in the paper. It looked like fun, but it's the same evening as my kids' fiddle lessons," Holly said.

"Well, they meet every week and have some coffee and cookies in the basement of the Lutheran Church. We buy a set of books that we pick out and we are each given two books a month to read. Then, once in awhile, the Reverend might ask us to give a short opinion on the story or tell the rest of the club what the book was about. Sort of like a book report at school."

"I didn't think Jack was much of a reader," Holly shouted over the hair drier.

"He's not. I had been asking Jack if he was reading his stories because I never saw him spending any time at it. If it's not Louis L'Amour or the newspaper, he usually doesn't read it. Well, wouldn't you know, the first person the Reverend asks to talk about his book is Jack. I don't know why he just didn't tell him he wasn't done reading, but you know Jack. He thinks he can B.S. his way through anything and proceeds to tell the entire *Christians of Cascade Book Club* - that *Farewell To Arms*, by Ernest Hemingway, is a book about an accident in a sawmill and *To Kill a Mockingbird* is a hunting story."

"No... Did he really?" Holly giggled.

"Yup. The whole line of bull, just like I said," Robin said lifting her eyebrows and frowning.

"Sheese'. What did the Reverend Johansen say?" Holly asked.

"Not much. He just rolled his eyes and clucked his tongue like a chicken. Nobody else said anything either, but I am too embarrassed to go back. I think we'll just join the Methodist Church.

They were both quiet for awhile.

"I already bought all the books for the club, though. Do you want some? They're in that box by your feet," Robin asked. pointing to the stack by Holly's feet.

Holly picked up the top book.

"Hmmm, this looks interesting. *Ancient Animal Traps and How to Build a Burmese Tiger Pit.*" She started smiling broadly.

Mark 3:25

Steve

Steve and Wilson seemed like they might be a bad fit. Wilson T. Huggs was an evangelist from Alabama and enjoyed a life of privilege. He appeared to have been pampered for most of his thirty-some years of age. He was a bit heavy and looked to be pretty soft. Steve was his absolute contrast and he was guiding him for us.

Steve and I had both worked on the same cattle ranch twenty-five years ago. He is presently a logger but has worked at a variety of outdoor jobs over the years. All of them physically demanding. He can shoe three horses in the time it takes me to finish one. Steve has helped us out on the ranch or guided our clients over the years when we were short-handed. We paid him, but I never thought he cared about the money and mostly did it as a favor. I always suspected he secretly just enjoyed tormenting me and abusing our hunters.

It was about the third year I knew him, and on a winter morning that a big black horse blew up with him. We had all our winter clothes on and Steve wasn't expecting a bronc ride. On about the second jump, the horse got Steve out over the front end to the point where he had his face right in the horse's mane. It figured he was a goner. Steve just hooked his heels under the cantle and bear-hugged that horse's neck with such force that his eyes bugged out. The horse's did, too.

I suppose riding that bucking horse with the saddle horn pounding into his chest didn't feel too good, but the horse got tired of the deal before Steve did, and he rode him to a standstill. I would have really enjoyed teasing him about his unconventional technique, but Steve was now in an extra bad mood and I surmised it might not agree with my health. I wisely deduced that anyone who could choke down a thirteen hundred pound horse as raunchy as Black Jack with his bare hands probably wouldn't have much trouble with me.

"Gosh, that's a tactic you don't see much," I said.

"Not too pretty, but effective. He always was a goofy sonovabitch. There aint' anybody takin' pictures around here anyway. Let's get goin,'" he snapped.

We are both busy with life and work these days so I usually only get to see him in the fall when he comes to help. At least once each season he would tell me:

"Please, fire me so I can get the hell out of here. Your hunters are gonna' drive me nuts, and I'm gettin too old to be draggin' these elk around."

He always starts out the day moderately grumpy and through the course of the day his mood deteriorates to somewhere between surly and outright murderous. He takes hunting very seriously and politically leans way to the right of Rush Limbaugh. His hunters usually got game, and that's why I paired him up with the least-experienced client.

Wilson had never been big game hunting before. His first of many infractions was when he reported for duty sporting a crispy new Cabella's matching pants and coat ensemble of blazing orange.

"My God, they could see you from space," Steve said. "Leave those pants here if you're going with me. The coat is bad enough."

Wilson looked at his coat.

"Ah' didn't know quite what to buy for this hunt. I've neva' been elk hunting before, so I bought a lot of gear for the trip. This is the only coat I have here though," Wilson explained.

"I'm gonna' need sunglasses just to look in your direction," Steve said shaking his head.

Wilson ripped open the Velcro keeping his pants on and took them to his room.

"We'll just have to try to stay out of sight," Steve said.

When Wilson came back out with denim jeans on, Steve added. "One thing to remember about elk hunting *you can fool their eyes, and sometimes their ears, but never their nose.*"

They drove the pickup on to a high ridge and glassed most of the morning without seeing any elk. When they did spot some, they were way off to the south with no way to drive any closer so they left the truck and took off on foot.

"Now walk right in my steps behind me. Pretend you're tracking me and step right where I step, and take those loose shells out of your pocket. You sound like Santa's sleigh." Steve took a deep breath and adjusted his day pack with his thumbs that were under the shoulder straps. "I'll watch the elk and keep the ridge or some trees in between us. When you get too tired, I'll wait; we've got all day, but let's hustle a little."

"Let us go unto the wilderness to smote the mighty wapiti," Wilson said.

Steven turned and looked straight into Wilson's eyes, "I smote a hunter once who got behind because he was screwin' around and not keeping up. Let's get goin."

Steve set a brisk pace and in about a hundred yards Wilson was fifty yards behind. Steve glowered at him when he finally puffed up beside him.

"I thought you said we've got all day?" Wilson huffed.

"I thought you said you could walk. We've still got to get there before dark," he hissed softly. "And you're making too much noise."

They eventually came in behind some trees, downwind, about eighty yards away.

"Where should I aim? Wilson asked.

"Lean on that tree and shoot for the middle of his shoulder when he clears those cows, if he does. Otherwise don't shoot," Steve shook his head doubting Wilson understood his instructions and said, "Just wait till' I tell you and don't move around so much. He's a pretty nice bull."

"I don't want to waste any meat. . . Should I aim for the heart?" Wilson asked.

"No!" Steve wanted to yell but stifled his anger. "I've seen more meat wasted because the whole elk got away than any other." Looking straight at Wilson's, he instructed, "I've done this a lot. Now hit him square in the shoulder. That three hundred you're shootin' will knock him down and he'll stay there."

They waited for the shot.

"Line the cross-hairs up just behind the front leg and aim for the middle of his shoulder. Shoot anytime. He'll go down right there," Steve was quietly pointing where the elk would fall.

The elk continued walking and feeding.

"How about in the neck?" Wilson asked as he held his gun without shooting.

"No, in the shoulder. It's not gonna' get much better. So shoot the first chance you get. . ." Steve was obviously getting frustrated but tried to remain calm and explained. "It's a lot better to knock em' down than havin' him hump up and go over the ridge to die who knows where. Besides I can get the pickup in here. He's sure in the clear now. Take your time but hurry up."

"Should I get out my range finder?" Wilson turned to Steve and asked.

"Shit no. Just shoot him. Now….shoot," Steve said practically hissing, and clenching his fists.

"I can't find him in the scope," Wilson said.

"You've got to hurry a little. . . their feedin' off. What power do you have that on?"

Steve looked and saw that the scope was on sixteen power.

"Turn that all the way down to four or six, as low as it goes. Four power is like lookin' through a window. Sixteen is like trying to find em' through a pin hole."

Steve's face fell as he watched the bull walk unscathed into the timber.

"Do you think they'll come back?" Wilson asked.

"I doubt it."

"Why don't we just follow them into the trees?" Wilson asked.

Steve shook his head and exhaled, "We'd have a Chinaman's chance. They're movin', they'd probably see us, and the odds are the bull wouldn't be in the back where you could get a shot at him anyway, especially as fast as you shoot. No one is gonna' move these elk if we don't. . ." Steve wanted to shake him, but he kept his cool and glassed the high ridge behind them for other game. He then patiently explained. "There's no one else in here. If we don't spook 'em, they'll be around to hunt tomorrow, and that's a nice bull. Let's start back to the truck Quick Draw. . . We should have killed that elk."

"I spoke to the Lord this morning and he told me, *there shall be tribulations*. Don't worry, brother Steven, I'm sure you'll do better tomorrow. . . Why does that shoulder shot work so well anyway?" Wilson asked.

"*I* did just fine, and it only works if *you* pull the trigger."

They continued climbing back to the truck in silence. When they started driving back to the lodge in the old white pickup, Steve started talking to Wilson again.

"I think the shot works because these animals are mostly water, and the hydraulic shock of it kills them. A bullet with all that power like yours puts all its energy into the hill on the other side of him if you just shoot through the ribs and miss all the big bones.

Up in the shoulder is the scapula. It's about the size of a football and the big leg bones are there, too.

When you hit one of those larger bones, I think the energy goes through the whole elk. The shock of it usually knocks em' down. Once they go down there's a lot better chance they'll stay there. I have seen em' take a lot and still get away. . .They're pretty tough."

When they got back to the lodge, Wilson went to his room and Steve relayed the day's events to me.

"He was dressed like The Great Pumpkin; and when we got ready to shoot, it looked like he was tryin' to mix a cake with the end of his barrel. Where did you get *this* guy?"

"He just called up, heard about us from someone, I guess," I got up from the big wooden table in the kitchen of the lodge and went over to pour us each a bourbon on the rocks. I set the brownest one in front of Steve and continued. "Now, don't piss him off or, worse yet, make him cry like you did that skinny bow hunter three years ago," I said.

"You mean that twinkle-toes from San Francisco?"

"Ya. That guy left in the middle of the night without payin' for the rest of his hunt. He still owes me two grand," I told him shaking my head.

"Two grand! . . . A guy beat me out of a two hundred one time, and he's still handcuffed to a pipe in my basement. That reminds me – I think I might've forgot to feed him before I came up here. . . Oh well."

Steve smiled and took another drink of his Jack Daniels before he finished his explanation.

"I was just teasin' that San Francisco guy and he couldn't take it. . . All I said was that his cammo' patterns clashed. . . Oh, and then I told him that all the elk scent that he had doused himself with was so strong it made my eyes water."

"I know some guys get a little carried away with that stuff," I said smiling to myself.

"I remember that day," Steve went on. "The guy told me, *this is the brand of elk urine that all the best archers are using this year.* **Cow in Season**, *and it's highly recommended in Bow Hunter magazine, too. A four stars rating.* Then he got all misty and his face paint started to run." A frown came over Steve's face and he said, "I don't think I got a tip from him either."

"At least he didn't try to run you through with an arrow. That lady fly fisherman, woman, whatever, you had out for me on the river, did her best to skewer you with her fly rod, and she even bragged about it," I said.

"That wasn't my fault. You knew I was no fly fishin' guide when you hired me. I just filled in to be nice and I was confused with all the names of those flies you gave me that morning to use on the Missouri by Craig that day."

"Well, it was her first and last time fishing, and I'm pretty sure she's never gonna' book again," I said.

"Good. You don't want er'. She was kinda' testy anyway. Right from the start. She kept getting' her line tangled up and said it was my fault for the way I was rowin'. I was dodgin' her hooks all day. She couldn't cast for sour owl shit, and I wound up with a Bead Head Nymph in each ear. I had to leave em' in there, too, till we got off the river, and then Danny Hamann down at the Driftwood Bar got 'em out for me that night. . .

I think where things really went South with that lady is when we got in a brawl over the flies she was usin'."

Steve reached up to feel his left ear for the old scar and then he rubbed it.

"I heard that, but I never did quite understand what really happened," I questioned.

"The way I remember, I think I told her she had a P.M.D. and she might have misunderstood what I ment'. Like I say, it was windy and all. Then I asked her if she'd tried a Wolly Bugger lately," Steve shrugged his shoulders.

"Are you sure you said P.M.D.?" I asked with no small amount of suspicion.

"Well, I'm pretty sure. And you can't believe how hard it is to escape from a determined two-hundred-pound Pilates instructor who's whipping at you with a fly rod inside the confines of a drift boat. She marked me up pretty good." He looked off and rubbed his left ear again while nodding to himself. "I should've got hazard pay for that one," he said.

The next morning Steve, Wilson and I were glassing from the truck on a ranch road. Steve was driving and Wilson was standing by the truck with the back door open and the window down. He had his elbows hooked over the opened window frame to help keep his binoculars steady. A nice five-point bull that a hunter on a neighboring ranch had kicked up, happened to run off the open hill in front of us about a half a mile away. We thought we could get Wilson a shot if we got up to the point on the road where the elk was going to cross. Wilson had not seen the bull because he was still looking through his binoculars in another direction.

Nor did he understand the urgency of the situation when Steve said '***let's go***'. It was kind of like hooky bobbin', except that we were dragging Wilson by his toes and he was using his arm pits to keep his torso securely in the window frame.

Even after two years there are still deep grooves in that part of the road and ugly finger nail scratches on the side of my truck. I hoped mightily that Wilson did not have any personal injury lawyers as close friends or relatives.

"When I say 'let's go,' I mean 'let's go' right now," Steve said sternly and too loud.

I thought Wilson was an awfully good sport. Even though he was way out of his element and five thousand feet higher than his home, he was trying hard. I wondered how well I would do at his job or in his city.

On a windy afternoon two days later Steve had Wilson set up on the east side of a timber patch.

"Now I'm going to circle around and come right through the timber. Whatever's in there should come out in front of you," Steve reminded him.

"How long should I wait?" Wilson asked.

"Until I come get you, and don't shoot me by mistake either. That'll really piss me off."

Steve circled around until he was on the opposite side of the timber and started working back and forth. That way he would be sure to send whatever elk there were out in front of him. He was two thirds of the way through when he heard a shot. *One shot always a good sign.* He thought. He arrived at Wison's stand to see that he had blood all over his eyebrow and right cheek.

"Did you get him?" Steve asked.
"I don't know. He was pretty close at first but by the time I assembled my shooting sticks he was up on the ridge. I aimed right for the shoulder," Wilson said

"How many were there?"

"Just the one I shot at, but he had pretty big horns," Wilson said.

"Good grief, you guys and your shooting sticks and all your damn stuff. You know I took all that crap away from my last hunter until the end of the trip. He was always messin' with his gadgets instead of payin' attention. . . You scoped yourself pretty good, didn't ya?"

"Yes, I think I cut my eyebrow. He was uphill and the scope hit me when I shot. Do you have any first aid supplies?" Wilson asked.

"Probably, let's go look to see if you got him, then we can tape that up."

"I think I may need stitches," Wilson whined.

"Na. . . It's a long ways from your heart," Steve said.

"My doctor said I have a very low pain tolerance, and my hips have been hurting like fire, too, from all this climbing. Do you have anything for pain back at the lodge?" Wilson asked holding his hand to his hip, slumping that direction.

"Sure. We always keep some bute around for the horses that we get from our vet. In case one of 'em comes down with colic or gets banged up. . . I think the whole name is Phenyl Butazone. It's great stuff, takes care of almost everything except warts. I've been usin' it for years. . .You look to be about a five CC man," Steve said.

"Horse medicine! But I've got a bad heart," Wilson winced sharply and held his hand across his heart.

"Oh hell, that's okay; it'll fix that, too," Steve said seriously waving his arm.

"Well, maybe. . . I don't really feel that bad right now, so let's just wait and see."

When they got to where the elk had been standing when Wilson took his shot, Steve started scouting for tracks.

"We'll see if we can find any blood," Steve said. "Don't walk around here too much. Just stand still so you don't disturb the ground. The way you're bleedin' I won't know if it's his or yours."

Steve was bent over, walking very slowly scrutinizing the ground and the elk tracks. He was following them up the hill away from Wilson.

"I am starting to feel a bit lightheaded from losing all this blood," Wilson said.

"You'll be okay. There's nothin' here anyway," Steve said.

"I didn't hit him?" Wilson asked.

"I sure don't see any signs of damage. If he was bleedin' as bad as you are, he'd probably be pretty close. . . Next time maybe you ought to turn the gun around and try hittin' him with your scope. You might get an elk and probably do yourself less damage, too."

I asked Wilson when he was by himself that evening if he wanted me to pair him up with a different guide. I thought he might be happier with someone more lenient.

Wilson bent his head as if in silent prayer and then he said, "I feel . . . brother Steven and I are kindred spirits. . . I would like to finish this journey of the hunt with him, if that is possible."

"Okay," I said. "But sometimes Steve likes to switch around so he gets to know the other hunters, too."

I talked to Steve about this while we were skinning out an elk on the meat pole.

"Hell, I started with the guy, I just as well finish," he said. "I don't think any of your other guides will have any better luck with him than I am. Besides, I like the way the guy talks – kinda' like Oral Roberts or something. Let's try to get him a mule deer tomorrow. A lot of times these guys seem to settle down a little after they've shot something."

The next morning was our last day of the hunt with Wilson. We crept up on some deer in a steep draw with some scattered stunted pines. Wilson and Steve were set up in front of me watching a five-point mulie who was full in the rut and absolutely engaged in his band of does.

I believe we could have done a line dance on the ridge with pink pom-poms and I don't think he would have even looked up. As I remember, it was about a four-year-old deer. Even though we kill much bigger bucks, Wilson was excited. We were quite close to the deer and he was getting to use his shooting sticks. He was also trying out his rangefinder and new rifle. I could see him smiling while he squinted through the scope well off to Steve's left and slightly behind him.

Steve was not expecting Wilson to shoot yet or he would have moved out of the range of the rifle's percussion instead of glassing for other deer.

"Steve, you better move over more before Wilson shoots. It'll blast your ears," I advised.

"I know. Don't worry. I've got plenty of time and this deer's not goin' anywhere."

Bang - Wilson took his shot.

Steve's head rocked over and the deer collapsed simultaneously. Wilson was ecstatic and threw his bright orange hat in the air. In a moment Steve regained his focus and started looking through his binoculars at the spot the deer went down.

"Steve, did that hurt your ears?" I asked.

"Huh?"

"Did that muzzle blast make your ears ring?" I asked again.

He looked down at his wrist and said, "It's twelve fifteen."

Proverbs 16:32

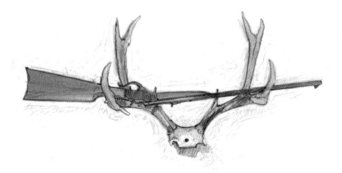

Aging Gracefully

There are a lot of advantages to getting older. People don't expect as much of me as they used to; also it's quite easy to find someone who time has devastated even more than it has abused me. People's memory is generally kind when it comes to the sins or inadequacies of my youth, and I am learning that the older I get the better I was. For instance, I rarely rode a really tough bull when I was competing. Now as I come to find out, I was actually quite sticky and seldom got bucked off. You can't imagine how happy that makes me. There are fewer people around now to dispute how often I got tossed, and the ones who are have failing memories. Most of them spend half their time trying to come up with some forgotten name and the other half looking for a place to relieve themselves. Thank God, there were no camcorders around then to document my abilities. At the present progression, if I live long enough, I might have once qualified for the N.F.R. I had a great time at those rodeos and the folks I met and all the fun I had were priceless. I never once put on a resume that previously I was a bull rider. Besides the experience, all I ended up with were a few trophy buckles and some arthritis.

I never turned down a bull, no matter how dangerous or how bad his reputation was. I got on and tried to ride every one of them, even if the bull couldn't buck much and his only goal was to maim you.

I thought it was a sign of courage to try them all, but now I think it was just stupid. Sort of like a boxer bragging that he never ducked a punch.

I don't see how some of those bull riders come back from the terrible injuries they endure. When I was competing, no one wore the protective vests or helmets like they do today. At a professional rodeo in Missoula, a bull landed in the middle of me after I got bucked off. The hoof went under my front ribs and broke four of the short ribs along my spine from the inside out. While I was in the hospital, I had time to re-access my priorities. I had ridden the same bull earlier that summer and won money on him, but obviously this time it was his turn. I got on a few more bulls later on, but like they say, it had *broke an egg in me*. I never craved it the same way again. Since I quit when I was quite young, it allowed me to focus on other agendas, like business and family responsibilities. As it ends up, it was a favor to me.

Time seems to have developed a sense of humor and is trying to find out how fast it can transform me into an oompa-loompa or maybe I'll morph into the cartoon character of George Jetson's boss, Mr. Spacely. Right now, I could be his stunt double. I believe I have about the same number of hair follicles as I used to but they seem to be migrating south. My wife's theory is that I'm so hardheaded that these follicles couldn't set down roots.

They are behaving like the folks around here that go to Arizona for the winter. Pretty soon my barber will want a finder's fee. These little deserters are leaving my crown at a disturbing pace and seem to be setting up camp in various embarrassing locations along their journey. By the time they all get to Florida, (or wherever they're going), I probably won't need to wear socks. My patchy hair is taking on the qualities of moss, and in general I seem to be getting kinda' fuzzy. Maybe I've spent too much time on the north side of a tree.

My arms are too short now to hold a cell phone at a distance that's within my range of focus. I hold it out as far as possible and randomly poke at buttons when it beeps, sings, or buzzes. I can never seem to remember the code for our voicemail either. If I don't locate the pocket that the phone is in by the time it quits ringing, I have no idea who called or what they want. It's difficult for me to hit just one of the tiny numbers even when I do see them. The whole process is very frustrating. I figure if someone really needs to get a hold of me, they will eventually write a letter.

What most concerns me is not my physical transformations, but I understand my temperament is eroding as well. I overheard my sons talking in the next room before they went to sleep last night.

"Can you believe he made me drive staples out on the fence by the road while I'm still on crutches?" Matt sighed.

"You've just been playin' X–box and watching T.V. all summer anyway, and I've noticed Old Iron Nuts likes to see a guy stay busy. A little work won't hurt ya. Gives you something to do besides eat chocolate ice cream. You know, they say you are what you eat. You're even starting to look like milk chocolate," Jake whispered.

Matt threw his paperback book at Jake in the dark, and it bounced off the wall.

"No, sir," he said. "You look just like Mom and I look like Dad. It's not from eating anything. What I've been thinking is - I don't think we even make minimum wage around here. It's like a prison work gang or something. Slave labor! We even have to pick rocks sometimes."

"Well, you'll be out in three more years with good behavior," Jake snickered.

"Couldn't I get worker's compensation or something? I was working for him when the horse fell on me. Don't they pay you for that?" Matt said.

"I don't think you can get that from your folks. I bet you have to have a regular job and pay taxes," Jake said.

"I'll tell you what I think. Did you see Dad's pictures from college? He had all that curly brown hair and that big Foo–Man–Choo mustache? Now his hair's getting shorter and his mustache is lots closer to his nose. By the time he's old he'll look like Hitler. I think he might be turning into a Nazi - **Ve haf vays uf makink you do da fensink**," Matt teased.

They got a good laugh out of that one and giggled themselves to sleep. I realized, then sadly, that I had transformed into a hard-ass somehow over the years without even knowing it. There is a great line by an anonymous author that reads, '*Our deeds travel with us from afar, and what we've been makes us what we are.*' I suppose that's how I've regressed to the present state. I sure didn't start out this way and I know I didn't mean to. I guess that there is just lots to do on a ranch with darn little time, energy, or resources to get things done. When we're sorting cows, it's:

"In" or "by"

– not -- "Oh, Katie, would you please use this window of opportunity to let in the little heifer, when you have a chance, that's speeding past your gate before she runs in with the rest of the herd of five hundred cattle, …and we have to spend all morning getting her back out of the bunch, …and we're so late that we can't load the trucks, …and we end up losing the ranch."

It's all kind of a hard business. It didn't happen overnight; but after years of dedication; I've achieved a reputation as - **The Head Hard-Ass** on the **Tough Shit Ranch.**

Oh vell.

Psalm 37:25

This book,

Dances with Hooves, is the most recent publication of the author, Skip Halmes. It is $10.95

A previous publication is entitled

The Cow Whisper, is $9.95.
Either of these books can be obtained from the publisher shown below.

(Please add $3.50 for S/H)

Call or write
      Quixote Press
    3544 Blakslee Street
    Wever IA   52658

    1-800-571-2665

For an autographed copy e-mail Skip Halmes

      shalmes@dadco.com

About the author

Skip Halmes is a Montana native with close ties to the land. He and his wife Holly raise kids, cattle, and a lot of dust.